This Journal Belongs To

The Sunflower Poets

my
he
you
my re
the one
at you are.

my renaisso
s, the one th
on and exhaled

...me breaks loose

p crashing. The tide is pulling me in.
...ping for breath, and feel that bone chill sink
...fall, but its not terrifying. It's quiet, peaceful an
...you are to me for the those dark day
...ilence isn't quiet, the air isn't in my lungs, and
...isn't in my heart there you are for me, all I will

...till, selfishly, I long for more—
...old you in my arms and feel you breathe in my embrace
...in my heart you will stay with all of the other ghosts.
...your voice forever intertwined with mine
...I couldn't forget you even if I tried
...For even the strawberries remind me of your chee
...How lucky am I

The Art & Poetry of Travelers

VOLUME ONE

by R. Clift

ROMA | MONTECATINI TERME | FIRENZE

2022

to my Sunflowers,

Federica, and Kristine

Post Card

For Correspondence

Address Only

Scan this QR code to visit a secret page on my website showing photos, videos, & more from our trip! You can hear my travelers sing in a castle, watch them dance through Tuscany, and see Italy through our eyes as if you were standing right there with us.

This Journal

Hi there, my name is Rachel— and you've stumbled upon our travel journal. In the summer of 2022, I gathered a group of artists to travel to Italy together with one goal— to capture what we experienced in art & poetry.

My travelers flew in from all over the world— Australia, Germany, Norway, Malaysia, & the U.S.— to join me and follow their own inner calling to explore and create.

Now, we call ourselves 'The Sunflower Poets', but we began as thirteen strangers. It only took a matter of minutes to feel like we we're long lost friends meeting up after so much time apart.

I've come to realize, something unexplainable and intrinsically cosmic happens when so many poets gather together to create and observe and allow themselves to be open and vulnerable— not only to the world around them— but to each other. Maybe it's in the nature of the universe to send inspiration towards those who are looking for it, but I swear, for the entirety of this trip, we couldn't stop writing. We were overflowing with words.

As this was my first time hosting an international artist retreat, I had no idea what to expect. I could only hope my artists would find poetry and beauty and friendship in our short time together.

What transpired was nothing short of pure magic. To this day— I have a hard time putting into words exactly what this trip, and these poets, mean to me— and what they now mean to each other.

Leigh, Catherine, Freydis, Cas, Benae, Jen, Emma, Mel, Malena, J.S., Kaitlyn, Laura— thank you for being my renaissance. Thank you for sharing your art & poetry here in this anthology. May the world be as in awe of your poetry as I am with each and every one of you.

May we, always, turn towards the sun.

Ever yours,

xx R.

ROUTE

Austria

Switzerland

Slovenia

Milan

Croatia

Turin

Verona

France

Genoa

Venice

Ligurian
Sea

Bologna

Adriatic
Sea

Montecatini Terme

Florence

Rome

Sardegna

Tyrrhenian
sea

Napoli

Bari

Cagliari

Mediterranean
Sea

Palermo

Ionian
Sea

Sicily

Itinerary

Day One - July 3rd:
- Arrive in Rome
- First dinner together
- Wander to Trevi Fountain

Day Two - July 4th:
- Travel to Tuscany
- Introductory Art & Poetry Workshop
- Explore Montecatini Terme together

Day Three - July 5th:
- Art & Poetry Workshop One
- Create art together in Tettucio Terme
- Pasta making class
- Dinner in Castello del Trebbio
- Evening stroll & stumble upon a symphony

Day Four - July 6th:
- Art & Poetry Workshop Two
- Travel to Florence & explore
- Meet Michaelangelo's David & his prisoners
- Impromptu dinner in Sante Croce

Day Five - July 7th:
- Impromptu 3 extra workshops
- Picnic in Parco Delle Terme
- Dancing in the rain atop Montecatini Alto
- Magic, Magic, Magic

Day Six - July 8th:
- Art & Poetry Workshop Three
- Visit & tasting at Brunello Winery
- Travel back to Rome
- Goodbye dinner & stroll to Trevi Fountain

Day Seven - July 9th:
- Final goodbyes & fly home

Via Bella Memoria

Travelers

Here, I would like to formally introduce our travelers, dreamers, & artists. Laura wrote a poem and sketched each of them, and I took their official author photos!

Laura Clift

I spent a week with eleven dreamers, poets who turned to me with leather bound pages, their eyes full of stars and eternal city lights and saying-

"I've spilled my ink- will you tell me what you see?"

— L.A. Clift

Cas McDowell

Cas

She is an explorer of the truest sense. Not only does she ask 'where next', she asks 'why'? She flies on warm winds, spreads her wings, eager to discover the next ancient land. If you can, take her arm, run, leap, and soar at her side. She will show you the creations of our world in a new light and open your eyes to the past.

CAS MCDOWELL

Catherine Pitts

Catherine

She is sunshine peeking through orange trees. The laughter carried on warm sea breezes, the clinking of an afternoon aperitivo. She is the playful voice suggesting 'gelato is always a good idea', the welcoming embrace of a long lost friend. She is sunflowers reaching for the light. She is the joy of Italy.

CATHERINE PITTS

Melissa David

Mel

She must have music. It's in the way she moves
through life, day by day, like a song yet to
be written. Or a song written each year, day,
moment- always renewed. She is the whisper of
birdsong in umbrella pines, the echoes of the
past in old castle walls. I have known her long
and yet, maybe not at all. Like a melody I once
knew well… she must be music.

MELISSA DAVID

Denae Terese

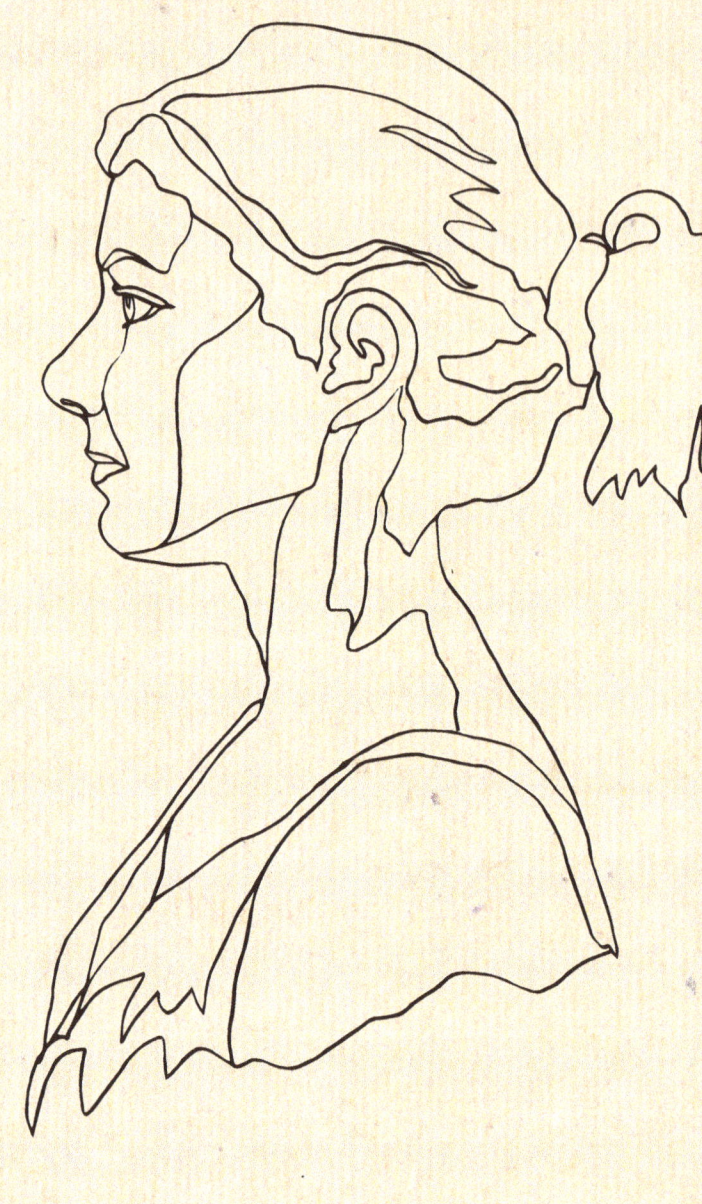

Denae

She is as constant as the sunset and as unique as the golden rays pouring over medieval towers, Tuscan villages, and dusty blue mountains. Her presence is as great as the sky and quiet as a birdsong. The beauty she is and the magic she creates- she is poetry.

Emma

The depths of the ocean could not fathom her.
She is still as glass— cool waters reflecting the
Tuscan sun— and yet, there is a force within her
that no one can define. Beneath the crystalline
laugh, the easy grace- is a beautiful tempest. A
presence, a voice that can call down the stars.

EMMA CONLON

Freydis Lova

Freydis

She calls to ancient souls and braids them slowly through her long umber hair. The Songs of Old course through the earth, into her veins, to the tips of her fingers. Every word, every verse she records harkens back to the time of Story. The time of voyages and myth and destiny. May you be fortunate to fall into her mythos.

FREYDIS LOVA

J.S.

J.S.

He is a secret library of handwritten words on pages, careful thoughts, and carefree conversation. A trove of poetry kept safely bound and protected. If you are patient and kind, you may be able to read a verse or two— be let into his confidence. There, he is true. He is brave. He is a poet.

J.S.

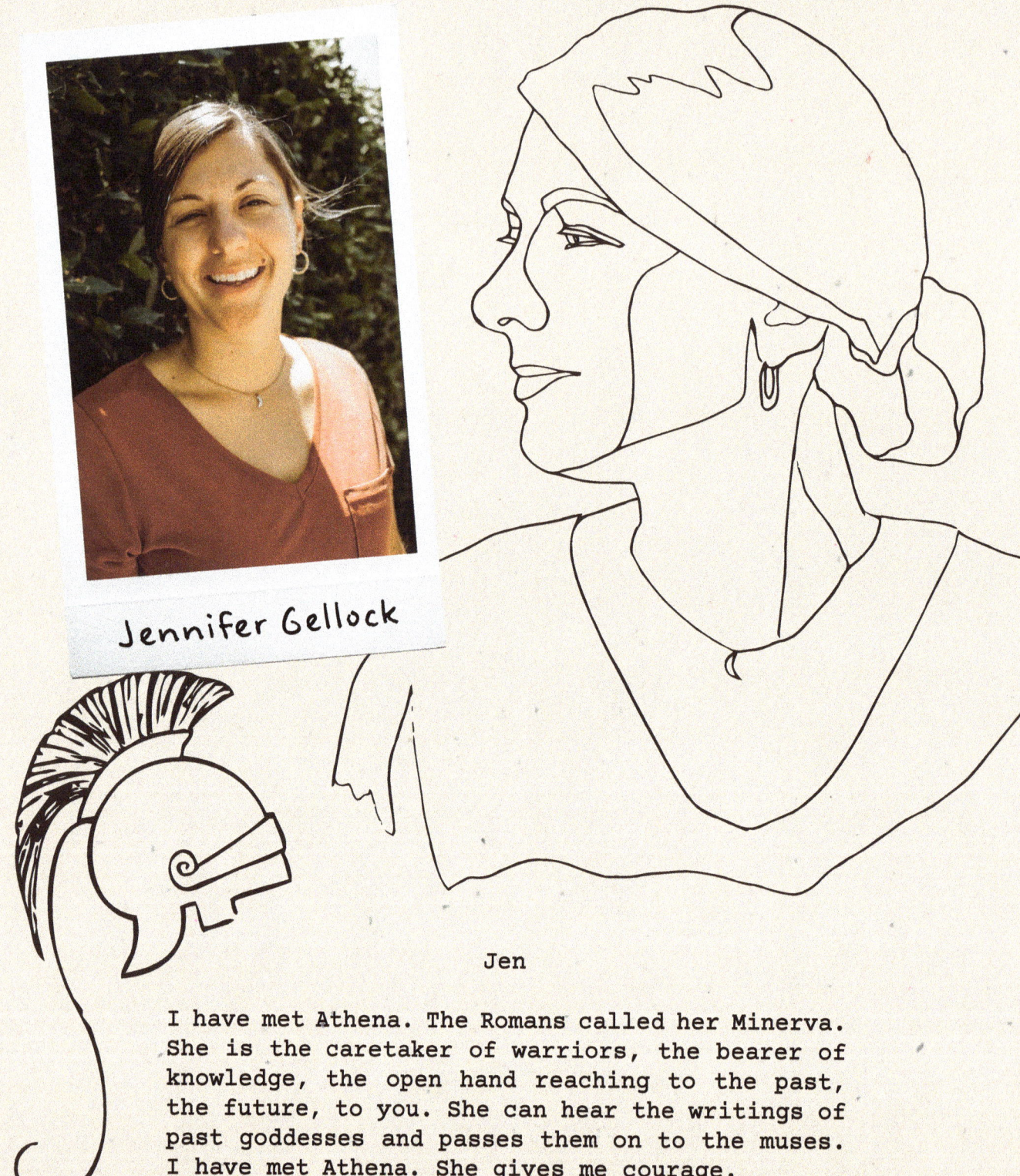

Jennifer Gellock

Jen

I have met Athena. The Romans called her Minerva.
She is the caretaker of warriors, the bearer of
knowledge, the open hand reaching to the past,
the future, to you. She can hear the writings of
past goddesses and passes them on to the muses.
I have met Athena. She gives me courage.

JENNIFER GELLOCK
———

Kaitlyn

She is the word you've been searching for. The solace of a poem just written. The delight of wandering cobbled roads and tall buildings warmed by the evening sun. She's the flowers unexpectedly around the corner, the orchestra music drifting by, the smile that matches your own. She is the word for belonging, for friendship, for home.

KAITLYN YÍNG YUÉ

Malena Grace

Malena

She is la luna, resting far above the noisy piazza, the brightness of a crescent smile. Even when she chooses to take shelter beyond the stars she holds the strength to change the tides. The balance of sea and land, unknown and familiar, new and ancient. A song older than time shines through her, happy and full— and if you're lucky, one evening stroll you may witness her light.

MALENA GRACE

———

XXIV

Leigh Fisher

Leigh

She creates dreamworlds in syllables and weaves
magic into paragraphs. The melody of the poetry
within her renaissance heart whispers among the
waters of Montecatini. A muse, a creator— she
takes in the world and all it has to teach her,
crafts tools to compose a fantasy between book
covers so intricate- you soon won't know the
difference between reality and dream.

LEIGH FISHER

Rachel

How do you pin down a constellation?

She is made of many stars. Blinding and
faint. Many words. Familiar darkness and
pinpoints of hope carefully strung into
intricate webs of mystery and truth for
the passing stargazer.

But you'll only glimpse the brightest.

For those willing to brave the longest
nights, she'll carefully drop the dimmest
starlight into your palm, hoping to the
moon you will catch it. Soft as a prayer.
A promise.

If you do, if you stay- you may be able
to finally know her as she is, in the
space between the stars.

- L.A. Clift

Rachel Clift

R. CLIFT

XXVI

The Art & Poetry of Travelers

We came across different seas,
admirers of the same sun.
We came with separate stories,
prepared to write on the same pages.

Together we laughed and cried,
we wrote from inspiration,
from marbled art to new smiling eyes.
Us, poets, from different lands...

We created this book,
The Art & Poetry of Travelers
which now has somehow landed in your hands.

Between each page is a conversation,
a laugh, a memory shared, a moment held.
What will you do with the stories untold?

These stories will be forgotten by all except the wind.
The same wind that moves across the pages of this book,
holds the magic and passion that was found in our trip.

It holds the transcript of the world,
the messages from the wind,
and the lyrics from within.

This wind is with you now,
let it move you.
Let inspiration cause something buried within you,
to bloom.

Because you my friend,
have a pen or pencil waiting for you.
There's art waiting to be made,
only destined to be signed by your name.

You hold *The Art & Poetry of Travelers*
but you are the traveler,
the poet,
the artist.

Be bold —*your story deserves to be told.*
This world is waiting
for your touch, your words, and your love.

- Catherine

July 3rd

Arrive in Rome

I met my traveler's for the first time tonight for dinner! I must say I was a bit nervous, not quite sure what to say— but they softened all my nerves with their smiles.

After spending the morning in Villa Borghese, we met up with our tour guide, Federica (who is incredible!) and gathered with all my travelers in the lobby of our hotel.

I could see it in their eyes when they saw me— "She's real!" "She's taller than I expected!" and I wonder what they read behind my eyes. Could they tell I was terrified? I handed out their journals— of which I wrote personal letters in the front & they seemed to really enjoy them. I hope they'll be creating and writing in them all week! I can't wait to get started. My sunflowers back home have started blooming today, I wish I could be there to see them in person— but I'm sure we'll see sunflowers soon on our way to Tuscany.

At dinner we had cacio e pepe pasta, chicken & veggies, and my favorite— tiramisu. Listening to stories and watching my travelers begin to form connections is one of the greatest joys. After dinner— we didn't want the night to be over— so my sleepy travelers walked all the was to the Trevi Fountain together.

They all tossed a coin in, assuring their return to Italy. We laughed and smiled and it was just a perfect evening in Rome.

R. CLIFT

There is only one way:
find the impetus that b...
Does it stretch out its...
heart? Can you avow...
forbidden to write? Abo...
...ask yours...
for a true...
...ould ring ita...
...can conf... ...ny meet this serious questi...
..."I must," then build your life upon i...
...your necessity. your life, in even th...

July 3rd

IT WAS A BRIGHT, HOT DAY IN THE ETERNAL CITY OF ROME. ITALY, SPECIFICALLY in July, has the same energy as a little town adorned for a festival. The buildings are more cheerful, colorful, and open. People strike up conversations, stroll along together, and take in the cerulean blue skies under multicolored strings of laundry strung across like flags. Music drifts from places that have been too quiet through the bare winter and rainy spring. As the fuschias and azaleas beckon to the golden rays, so does Italy to those who wish to explore.

Our adventure began in a suitably transitory space for a group of travelers, artists, and poets to first meet. The lobby of the Hotel Regio, a stone's throw from the Termini Train Station.

The lobby itself was all veined marble, warm ivory walls, and forest green accents. The front door was guarded by two pale stone lions lazing on parapets, obviously not sensing too much to be alert to.

First, Rachel and I met our local guide, Federica, who would shepard us through the Tuscan countryside during the next week. She was tall, direct, elegant- not unlike the umbrella pines we had visited in Villa Borghese that morning. The trees held a cloud of foliage above them like a line of ballerinas reaching to the sky. Federica's presence called back to their grace and magnitude. I knew instantly our journey was trusted to capable hands.

We met our eleven travelers across the long lobby in an out of the way alcove with golden wall sconces and bright yellow couches. This moment was one of the most astounding— after months of planning, communicating, preparing— here we all were. Fourteen people with long unique days behind them, many more ahead, with their own childhoods and failures and favorite TV shows— were now situated together in a small cool room on an afternoon in Rome. Everyone was buzzing with possibility, excitement, and a healthy amount of anxiety that caused a burst of giggles every now and then during our introductions. After all, fear and freedom feel a lot alike.

In a few short days we would know one another well and look back on these first moments with cheerful relief and astonishment.

"Can you believe we were strangers five days ago?" someone would say.

"But were we, though?" another would reply.

Now, as a newfound merry band of travelers, we traversed the Roman roads to have dinner at a small restaurant called *La Lupa*. A long table spread with white cloth and adorned with shining plates and green glass bottles awaited

I

us in a corner by the open windows. We settled into our seats and over the course of the evening, into each other's company.

Over the first course of cacio e pepe, a traditional pasta dish of simple but quality ingredients, we all spoke of similarities, differences, passions, and origins. We shared sweet white wine, hearty red, and funny stories from our arrivals and journeys to the hotel. There was roast chicken and vegetables and talk of what was to come.

A comfortable sort of anticipation hummed between us all. Once the last bite of tiramisu was gone— we were all ready to discover what the week held for us. I was already fascinated and half in love with each of the incredible artists sitting at the table. With days to hear their stories and make memories of our own— I felt extremely grateful for the privilege.

We were too enraptured in conversation to go straight back to our rooms— so we all decided an evening walk was the ticket. The heat had fallen beyond the horizon as evening stretched on and Rome was left in a warm, comforting blue haze. The citrus trees grew still as the winds turned in for the night, and although the walkways, cafes, and shops were still bright— so were the stars. The twilight beckoned to be shared among new friends.

We ventured out through large cobbled piazzas, passed fountains, wide open roads strung with small blue and red cars, and through winding back streets framed on either side by flat neutral buildings with their shuttered eyes facing one another. Stone steps between streets were slippery with the thousands of shoes that had polished them over time. The sweetness of window-box flowers drifted with the earthiness of damp pavement as our laughter and questions of *how far until we turn left?* mingled with the late night diners ordering supper at the sensible hour of ten o'clock.

We were drowned out completely as we turned into the relatively small square where the illustrious Trevi Fountain stood proud and indifferent before a large bustling crowd. The massive sculpture was situated at the base of a small amphitheater-like plaza. Small streets branched off along the edges of the shops, gelaterias, and offices. The space was intended for passersby to take a break from grocery shopping, or a meeting point for friends on bicycles to find one another. Instead, this fountain, of more than 300 in Rome, became a major sight to see and the small square seemed all the smaller for the amount of people.

All eyes were on the almost iridescent figures hovering over the sea-glass blue water. Our group gathered close, quickly coordinated a plan, and set off in a single line through the masses of families, couples, and young people to the

II

far right corner where the crowd petered off and we could have a moment to hear each other.

There was only one thing to do, of course, we agreed. Coins *must* be tossed into the water. We fished in wallets, bags, and pockets until an assortment of currencies were presented to each empty hand.

"Doesn't matter what kind of coin," someone said. "A wish is a wish."

We took upon this duty quite seriously. In pairs we shuffled to the fountain's edge, laughing at ourselves, only to check again about which shoulder was the proper one to throw the coin over. "I saw it in a movie— right hand, left shoulder." Right hand, left shoulder was repeated studiously before each wish. After a couple of us had completed the Roman tourist ritual, we began to accrue a cheering audience in the shape of a giddy Irish family of about nine people. Each time one of us successfully tossed a penny of various origin into the awaiting water— we were greeted with the proud whoops of the uncles, mothers, and children of this family. We befriended them and they even asked to hear one of Leigh's poems, which they enjoyed as much as the cheering. The hilarity was infectious and by the last pair of us we had the major portion of the right section of Trevi joining in on the fun.

We took photos and videos to giggle at later and at some point a couple of our travelers spotted the small fountain with two opposing spouts nearby designed to be drunk from by two people holding hands. Obviously, we had a go. Trying to drink from the fountain was much like attempting the same with a garden hose on full blast. The desire to maintain a "serious and important traveler" facade was thankfully shed away after a selfie with our new friends from up north.

This resulted in another round of laughter, quite a bit of sputtering, and the ease that grows among new friends when attempting silly feats together. We took a few moments to wipe our chins on our wrists and watch the seagulls land and alight from the magnificent, ancient fountain, before heading back through the blue and gold streets.

Italy itself was much like this night. Real, sometimes silly people going about life while surrounded by extraordinary beauty and ancient works of art. History and poetry in hand with friendship, laughter, and humanity— seem to all be an eternal truth.

III

07.03.22

printed in Italy

I 113   **Rome, Italy**

The Eternal City and Capital of Italy— Rome is one of the most iconic destinations in the world. A whirlwind of ancient history and vibrant modern culture— you'll find incredible art, haunting ruins, and delectable food.

Timeless icons such as the Colosseum, Roman Forum, and Trevi Fountain are all within a lovely stroll about the town. The ancient roads that branch across the country and beyond, one way or another, call most travelers in to find their way to the center of Italy.

Edizioni D'Arte I.F.I. Firenze
Riproduzione vietata

I don't know what made me do it—
the booking for this trip was posted online,
and I didn't hesitate.
For mavbe the first time in my life I did something
without thinking about it for days first.
Without turning it over and over in my mind,
wondering if it's the right choice or not—
worrying about all the things that could go wrong
Something pulled me towards Italy, and I let it.

I've always believed in magic, but somewhere along the way
I forgot that it can reach me too.
It felt like magic was reserved for other people,
and I was left with only the dream of it.
It was a fantasy, and truthfully I had lost my hope for it.

Here's the thing about it though; *magic is always there.*

Your eyes get used to the dark
and you forget to look for the stars,
but let me tell you—
they're still there.
The stars.
The magic.
The hope.
The cliche of it all is that
you have to look with your heart,
not your eyes, but I promise you—

It's all there.

— Malena ♡

Girasole in gabbia

Every facade fell away
as I took each step off the plane,
I don't recall a moment
I first lost my identity
or why my heart aches
a different way when I separate
myself from the mundane,
but underneath who I am supposed to be
breathes a girl I used to be,
Whispering a thousand lives
dreaming to be seen,
I would be naive to think
the outside world isn't a part of me
That its music plays a little quieter
with every sheltered heartbeat

Caged Sunflower

DENAE TERESE

11

I know them,

I thought, walking into the foyer of the hotel.

I know their eyes,

and the way their mouths turn up into smiles.

I know their laughs,

but I don't know their names.

Not yet, anyway.

But that's okay.

I'll learn them soon.

For now, knowing that we all share

the same dream is enough.

I still remember that moment
we all met for the first time—
within minutes— we realized we
were (somehow) old friends.
Some nights just make you believe
a little more in magic.

— R.

FREYDIS LOVA

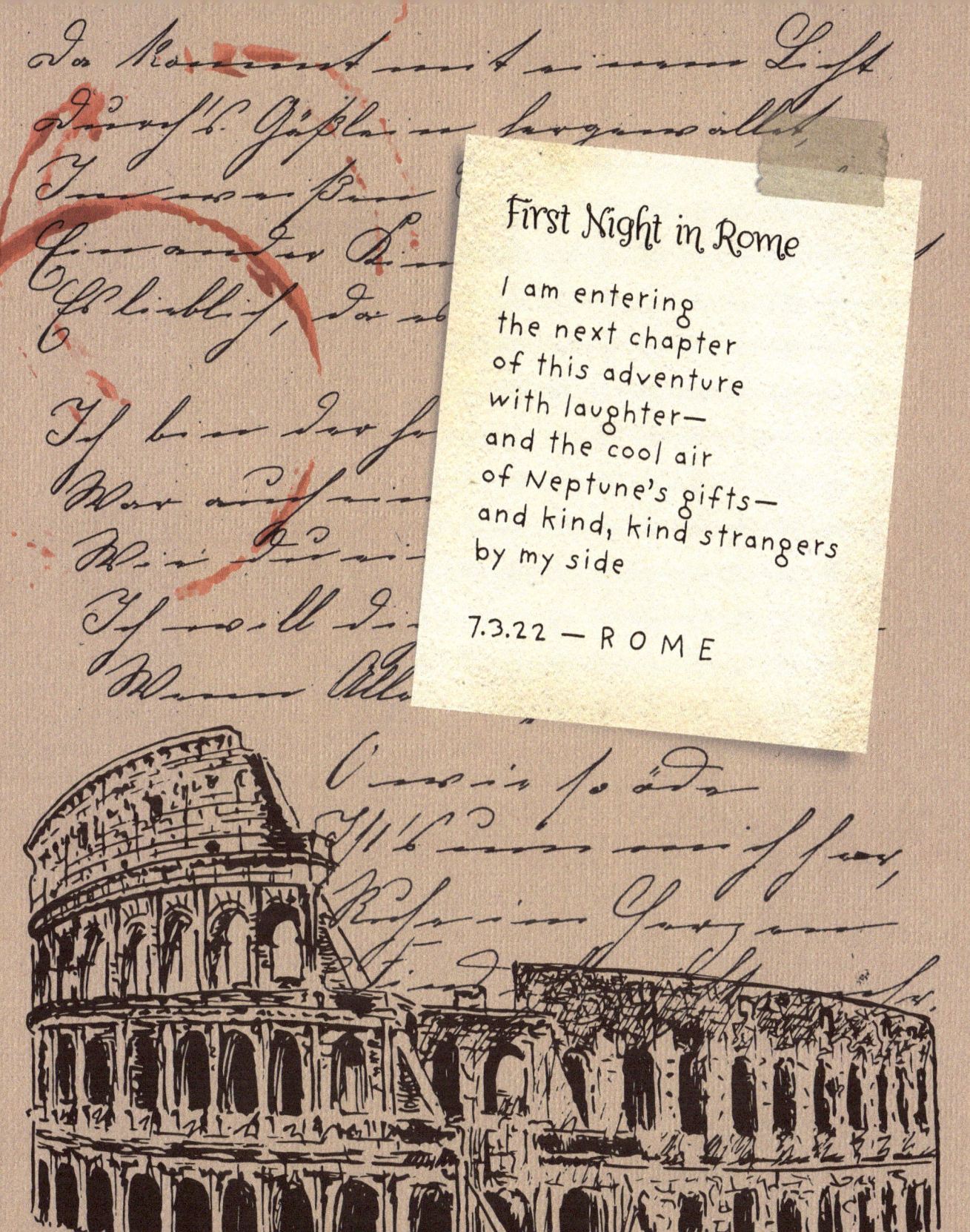

First Night in Rome

I am entering
the next chapter
of this adventure
with laughter—
and the cool air
of Neptune's gifts—
and kind, kind strangers
by my side

7.3.22 — R O M E

LEIGH FISHER

Oolaroo

Dreaming of the red dirt
Still stuck in my suitcase.
Even though I never traveled there,
I can feel the heat
And hear the creek
Of the aboriginal didgeridoo
Blowing through the endless
Desert wind pushing my feet.
I've never been there,
But the red sand
Still lives in my suitcase,
And it always makes me think of you.

Skeleton Key

How do I lock this door?
I sit, childlike,
staring at an ancient door,
grasping my skeleton key.

I fit it in,
turning it once
to a satisfying click.
It's still not locked. I say— starting to grin.
I turn it again and it starts
to move like Gringotts.
Four more times I turn the key.

Now, safely locked,
I remove the key,
smiling on the inside.
In true discovery, *childlike*,
I bear climb the thin stairs
to grab myself an victory drink.

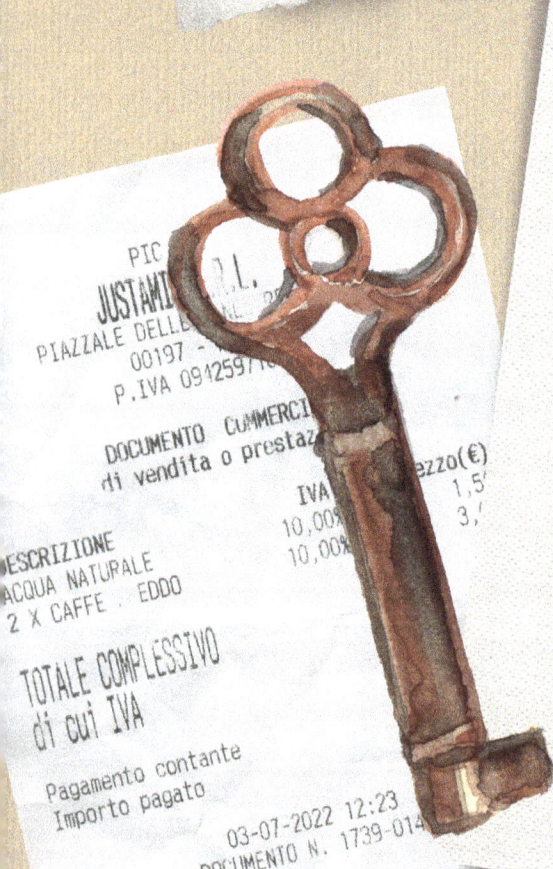

MELISSA DAVID

Back to Roma

Sundays are quiet in the city of Roma. A day of rest for the millions who bustle through weekday tiny streets. In the quiet, tourists can be found hearing their whispers carried through the city that holds both ancient secrets and modern dreams of love. Jet-lagged spirits wind down tight corners to the Trevi Fountain, tossing coins to cast new visions of their futures. In parallel timelines and alternate universes there wishes are coming true— returning us all back to the city of Roma— one day in the not so distant future.

Dear Roma, thank you!

My intentions before making my wish written down in my notebook.

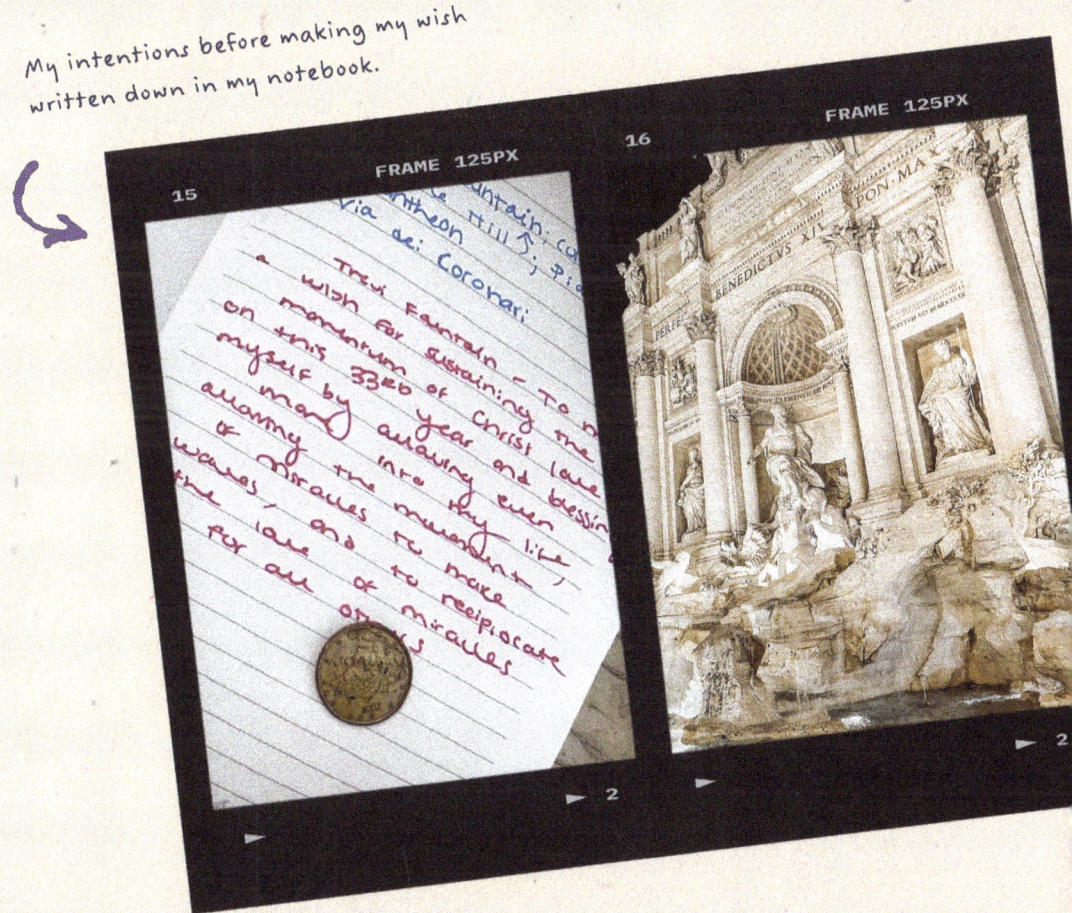

I.   *Lost… Again*

We exist in places where
we think we will eventually be heard
and found.
We discover things
we believe will lead us to the plan
we laid out.

Wandering along the way,
we weave in and around.
The future ahead tangles hearts
and minds linked to the past
we were hoping to shut out.

Lost in this place.
Lost again along the way.
Lost to remember the person
We were reaching for someday.

At times we get lost again,
Always shocked to realize
We have always been
Found.

CAS McDOWELL

That which I write has already been written,
in countless pasts and infinite futures.
I am simply a traveler
rediscovering it on my journey.

J.S.

printed in Italy

I 113 *Trevi Fountain*

Built atop an ancient aqueduct, the legendary Trevi Fountain is a breathtaking sight to behold. Legend says, if you throw a coin into the fountain— you will return to Rome.

This may harken back to the ancient Roman tradition of tossing coins into water as offerings to the gods to favor their travels and help them return safely.

Edizioni D'Arte I.F.I. Firenze
Riproduzione vietata

trevi fountain

I know that you truly love me,
& I can tell you a million
       reasons why.
two days ago, I knew
       when your hand slipped
wordlessly into mine as we
walked the streets of sorrento,
& yesterday I knew on the peak
       of monte solaro.
today, I know you love me
       because,
even in the stupor of exhaustion
(limbs windblown sapling-drooping,
feet blistering in your new
       white shoes)
you walk the streets of rome
       with me
to make a wish at trevi fountain,
a wish for you, for me, for us.
yesterday I knew when you lowered
       on one knee
at the peak of monte solaro,
& today I know as you close
       your hand
over the coin I hold in my fist.
a wish, a low hum, whispered like
       midnight prayer—
the steady arc of the flipping coin,
       slow crescent,
golden moon against a daylit sky.
my breath catches with the glint
of our wish-coin,
       glittering in the twilight,
sparkling like that daylight water,
like the ring you put on my finger.

EMMA CONLON

an ode to my younger self

hello, my darling.
it's been a while.
have you been well?
i hope so.
do you remember
how we used
to sit in a corner,
afraid, bruised,
and shadowed?
i wanted to come back
and tell you,
my love,
all the dreams we
never dared to dream
came true.

i can feel the tears
welling up
in your eyes,
because they are
in mine too.

in this present
that we never thought
we could reach,
i'm sitting in the
shade of a tree
beneath a shining
roman sun.
i'm surrounded by
kindred souls
all of whom are here
with a purpose.

KAITLYN YÍNG YUÉ

22

best of all,
i'm sitting here with
a pen's tip pressed against
the pages of a journal,
writing.

at long last,
i have called to home
all the secret fragments
we had to hide,
and made them whole.
we've made it home.

KAITLYN YÍNG YUÉ

Each of my travelers recieved a custom Soothi leather journal!

I've hardly ever seen a group of poets' eyes light up more.

Italy 2022

My dear Catherine,

We made it, we're in Italy and we're surrounded by ancient ruins & endless inspiration. Doesn't it feel like a dream? Thank you for joining me on this journey, I'm so happy our paths have crossed in this lifetime! I'm so excited to create and explore with you here in this country I hold so dear to my heart. May you fill these pages with your thoughts, musings, art, poetry, triumphs, fears, & hopes — anything, everything! May your heart be truly seen, May your soul be known.

All my Love, xx Rachel

SOOTHI
CONTAINERS OF CREATIVITY

WWW.SOOTHI.COM | @SHOPSOOTHI

Catherine's journal with some flowers she found!

This is not a journal.

This is the catalyst and container for creativity and change.

This is a purposeful, universal object that physically, personally connects you to your greatest inspirations, aspirations, ideas – and to the world we all share.

@ShopSoothi
www.Soothi.com

I'd like to think the darkness inside me is only ink and when I'm hurting, it bleeds out into words worthwhile.

— R. Clift

Cas's Journal

"Your thoughts deserve a decent place to live."

—Arthur Smith

I wrote my late poetry professor's quote on the first page of each journal

For the duration of this trip, we had a local guide take us by the hand. Her name is Federica, and she used to write poetry too, once upon a time. She was invaluable to this trip and it wouldn't have been the same without her!

Federica

The powerful one,

who leads wanderers

and teaches them with

the stories from her own life.

She has so much to offer,

yet chooses when to give.

She sparkles like the Tuscan sun

as she points out the beauty of her land.

She has lived an engaging life

and encourages others to do the same.

She holds pearls of wisdom from ancient lands.

A world without Federica is a desert without sand.

CATHERINE PITTS

Have you ever run up uneven stairs?
Panting, your chest tight,
and the world spinning around you
as you try your best to balance?
Slipping on marble and gliding over
invisible footprints worn into the streets
by strangers you will never meet
but will follow anyway?

You should.

Find an absurdly tall and crooked staircase
in the middle of the road
and run.

Run as fast as you can
without looking down,
and throw yourself into the arms
of the closest statue
when you reach the top.

Fill your lungs with rebirth
and watch the lights go out,
until all that's left is a chiseled soul,
a half empty bottle of white wine,
and bare feet in a fountain.

FREYDIS LOVA

—————

28

> With but pen, paper, and passion
> all men become poets.
>
> J.S.

spaghetti with clams

the clams, adorned in their laurels of parsley,
unfold like small palms open in offering.
you twirl your spaghetti in your fork
as I try not to envy your meal, the meal
I ought to have chosen—I strayed for
a tryst of cacio e pepe. these days, I am trying
to be brave, if only in these inconsequential,
incidental ways—admittedly a small act,
but for now, for today,

                          it is brave.
your hands, scooting your plate closer:
take whatever you would like,

                    alwaying willing
to barter, to trade, to bend, to make
me happy. it is one of the small ways
you tell me you love me.

we walk three blocks for gelato,
trade bites
        of hazelnut
            & strawberry
            & pistachio.
I feel my soul unfold before you,

like a small palm open in offering,
        like the clams.

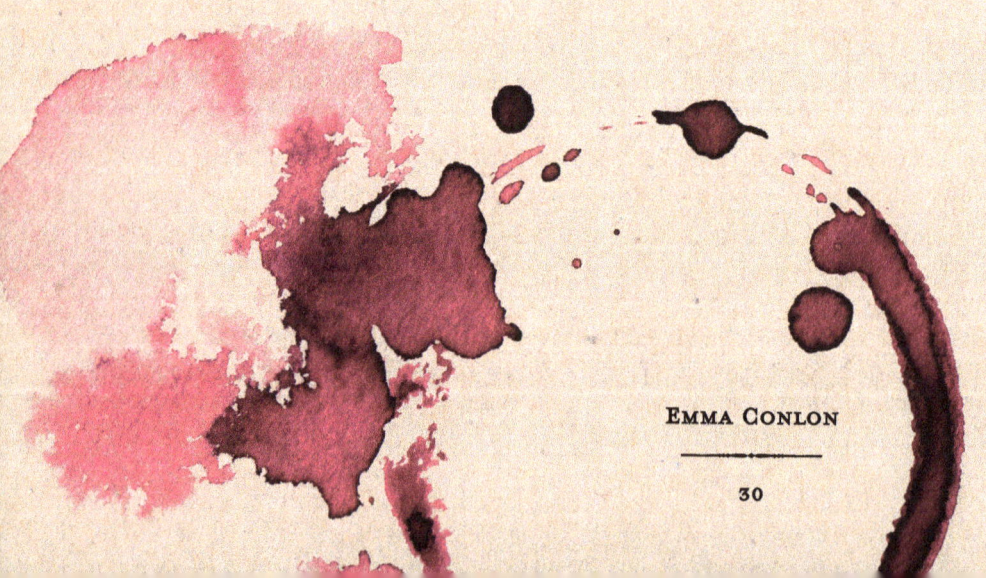

EMMA CONLON

My 30

I'm 70/30
And she is my 30
Long flowing hair,
The kind that never seems to need a brush.
Her olive feet peeking out of her
Dark flowing green pants.
Her matching crop top
Tortures me,
Covering only enough to make it appropriate.
She is effortless,
Learning a Tik Tok dance
In the living room
Laughing with a man I hope makes her happy.
My attention keeps flying past
The lively table full of wine to her.
My 30.

I'm not sure

Why is everything better in Italy?

Pasta, Wine, Cheese, Sex?

I'm not sure…

But everything is better in Italy.

MELISSA DAVID

Caged
is only
the limits
of this skin
– Denae Terese

3 for 50 euros

the velvet night cloaks rome in her satin skirts,
the kind of darkness that only choking, pin-hole
stars can poke through. these stars are not unlike
the ones we watch together on our balcony
a world away back in our other life—*the real one*,
we joke, a far cry from the storybook pages
we now waltz through.

                 the city sighs in relief
as july's flame is extinguished; all the marbled
columns and cobblestones can finally,
                 blissfully cool.
we pass the sundry tourist traps, carved into
the bottom floors of oblique buildings, tripping
over themselves and so alike in corresponding
tedium, the bland bubbling up from all the gaudy
trinkets. there is a kind of tantalizing sameness—
a glamor to the frivolous key chains, the cheap
misprinted magnets. the nearest shop's proprietor
is a stout italian man. his gruff demeanor is lined
with a warmth about the edges; he is happy
to usher us into his lair.
                 cheap knick-knack treasure
secured, we cross the misty gateway back into
our storybook. a return to the elysian world
we have come to know—we step over the threshold
and the city throws back her arms in welcome.
                 later,

we stop once more to admire
the watercolor paintings laid out
like tarot cards across the stones.
the artist tells us about art school.
how he's trying to make it out here
                 in this big, big world.
we wade through his curbside gallery,
pick 3 paintings: the trevi fountain,
the spanish steps, a bird's eye view
of the city from our storybook.

EMMA CONLON

3 for 50 euros. it hardly seems enough
we're all just trying to make it out here
                    in this big, big world.
I can't help but feel we too live
in the brushstrokes of a painting.
from above, another storybook girl
looks down on our sky, considering
if she will take us home, hang us up
on her living room wall. we too
oblivious to our newfound plane
of existence—the watercolor
blurring at the edges of our vision,
the soft margins of our bodies,
the way we blend and bleed.
                    meanwhile,

two people very much in love
look up to our painting, a recent
addition to the living room wall.
watch us pause our ambling to buy
watercolor paintings, *3 for 50 euros.*

how large the love can swell,
they say, *even in a place so small.*

EMMA CONLON

II.

Who are you writing for?

Yourself to release your soul.
Sharing it becomes a gift.

Because it is part of you.

Taken on the first
day in Rome

Taken on the
final day

CAS McDOWELL

3rd july, 2022

for someone who is nearly always late to everything in her life, the matter of importance is obvious when she ends up being the first one to arrive, for once. the power of sheer nervousness is real.

i just came back from meeting all of the group for the first time, and honestly, i'm still trying to catch my breath. we had only met in the evening for dinner so it was just a couple of hours overall but there was so much going on! i don't think i can describe it properly, but the weeks of nerves that i was having prior to this were so quickly replaced with a surge of ease and pure excitement. everyone seemed wonderful and i think i've already made friends with someone! she's super friendly and has red hair, it kind of reminds me of pixies. we went to the trevi fountain after dinner, and threw coins in for a wish. the night scene there was incredible, i've never seen anything like it.

July 4th

to Tuscany

Our first day in Montecatini Terme— a tiny jewel of a town in Tuscany, Italy. We drove through fields and fields of endless golden sunflowers. The word for sunflower in Italian is "girasole" and it means "to turn towards the sun". I'm aching to know the ancient secrets this place holds.

I taught my very first workshop on art & poetry— I only cried once when talking about my late poetry professor— Arthur Smith. I wrote his quote in the front of all their journals— just like I write in the front of mine: "Your thoughts deserve a decent place to live." They were taking notes in their leather bound journals while I was speaking, just like how I used to take notes in my journals while Art was speaking. [To deny your poetry is to deny the most honest parts of yourself.]

I talked for an hour about everything I have been dying to tell other artists for months. I read poems from "Voices in a Giant City" and "Letters to a Young Poet." At the end of the workshop— I had us all write exquisite corpses together. It's an old french parlor game where you collab together to write poetry. They always have a very magical way of coming together— but I didn't tell them this. I let them be skeptical so they would be even more pleasently suprised. It was quiet, while they were writing— I could tell they were apprehensive. I answered with a quiet, "Just trust me, and try."

As we read the poems out loud I could feel the energy in the room shift. From sitting down as a table of almost strangers— we were now a collective of artists and poets— tied together by our own exquisite corpses. This was the moment, for me, when the real and true work began. This is only the beginning.

R. CLIFT

...ffer order to remen...

...ry yet to be told...

...een lea...

...ver hold...

...hemselves were...

...st place to begi...

...be loved if I do n...

...my hands are shak...

July 4th

EARLY THE NEXT MORNING, AFTER A QUICK BREAKFAST OF STRONG COFFEE and apricot croissants, we met in the lobby with sleepy hellos and all of our worldly possessions in tow. Rachel and I had a few backpacks between us, and Federica only a small rolling bag. She looked at us and said appreciatively,

"The more you travel, the less you carry, yes?"

A great white coach bus, looking much like a space-ship parked on the old street, awaited us outside. There were more rows of burgundy red seats than there were of us. We each settled into our own space and met our driver, Nello, who hailed from sunny Naples. He was a stout quiet man with a deliberate sort of kindness. A small stuffed bear with a bow around its neck accompanied him on the dash, perhaps from a daughter or nephew back home.

We set off into the chaos of driving in Rome and I was very grateful we had such a skilled navigator at the helm. Small cars, compact utility trucks, and maniacal motorbikes buzzed around us. Our bus felt very much like a whale moving through a coral reef with small fish of all types swimming past with very important places to get to.

Federica took up the little microphone attached to the bus's radio and her voice resounded through the audio system.

She told us the history of streets and ruins, stories from her brief time living in Rome, and alerted us in the driest of tones whenever the bus had to make a quick stop that another idiot was on the road.

Once we were out of the city, everyone took a sigh of relief. It was all green fields, swaying trees, and azure skies beyond the highway. Towns clustered along the horizon and petered out into farms and country neighborhoods as we sped past.

The most spectacular sight of the drive was the masses of sunflower fields on either side of the road as far as one could see. They were harvested for oil, Federica explained. Waves of golden flowers broke against the hedgerows and cypress and silver-green olive groves.

"The word for sunflower in Italian is girasole. It means 'to turn toward the sun.'"

IV

L. A. CLIFT

As poets and romantics, this meaning increased the awe of the sight exponentially. Sunflowers, along with many other ordinary things, would take on such special meaning during our time together.

We made a couple stops at service stations for breaks to walk around, grab snacks, and get a sandwich or slice of pizza from a counter. They were interesting little spots both designed to be maneuvered through quickly and much like a maze. There were multiple entrances but only one exit— you had to pass through two shops that didn't quite look connected at first to leave. Impressively, we only set off two alarms when we happened upon the wrong exits.

The three hours passed by with magnificent views and friendly conversation. Book recommendations and favorite paintings were traded. New-to-us flavors of chips, sodas, and chocolates provided great distraction and discourse on our journey.

We arrived in Montecatini Terme on schedule, and just as the town was drowsing into its afternoon nap. Anywhere between one o'clock and four each day, as in most small Italian towns, the shops and businesses closed for a couple hours. Everyone went home for lunch before returning back to work. It seemed terribly logical, and it's something I still wish places back home might consider.

Arriving during this temporary, rather ghostly, period was much like driving onto a movie set. The tiny roads were stacked on either side with plain peach-toned buildings. Most of the deep brown and russet red shutters were closed against the day's heat. Shops with names in varying languages were quiet at street level. A few remained open with signs of life— the grocer, a gelateria, a laundromat. The rest would just have to wait until the day got a bit cooler.

Our bus sidled up beside the Hotel Tamerici Principe— an older turn-of-the-century hotel just off the main square of town. It was at least five stories with pale yellow walls, a fox red set of shudders, and a spray of various countries' flags adorning the front overhang. A dual red carpet stretched up the stone steps and led past the wide veranda that looped around the building into the lobby.

The whole place had a streak of delightful melancholy, more like a fancy hotel from a mystery novel than real life. The rooms were wide and vaulting. Our hotel keys weren't cards, they were metal keys with heavy charms engraved with the room number. Ornate mirrors hung before multitudes of arranged flowers, bronze statues of mythic figures, and spindly furniture. If the walls weren't

v

papered in stripes, they were floral, or gilded. The paintings seemed to all have been hung about a hundred years ago and never swapped out.

It had a sense of being forgotten over time, so much space for the relatively few people passing through. It was just as easy to imagine a jazz-age heiress rounding the corner as it was to find a French family on holiday enjoying the pool. It was colorful, embellished, and may once have been lively— but someone must have pressed a pause button ages ago and left the old movie on television.

We met for the first Art & Poetry workshop in the old ballroom only accessible by a single elevator in the center of the lobby. The room was wide and sunshine poured in through the windows lining the far wall. A bunch of little tables had been pushed to the center— each covered with its own green cloth— creating a patchwork of emerald.

Everyone was on time. In fact, quite a few travelers were earlier than us. Rachel stood at the end of the tables, kicked off her sandals, and spoke about how her love of poetry began. The story she has lived so far, the purpose of our trip, and much more.

We then hopped on the bus for a quick drive to the local restaurant Il Discepolo for dinner. As with most restaurants, all the tables were saturated outside under umbrellas and strings of small fairy lights. Orange trees with masses of glossy green leaves flanked the sitting area and sunny spheres of growing fruit hung around us like banners for a party.

Tonight's courses were seafood based with traditional preparations of the region. A salmon and veggie pasta, baked white fish, and macedonia con crema— mixed fruit with frozen whipped cream. It was the perfect, easy ending to a day of travel and I was happy to have another chance to get to know our companions and discuss the day's workshop.

We journeyed back to the hotel at sunset and a group of travelers branched off to check out a little place down the road— but Rachel and I needed to go scout for the next day's outdoor workshop. After a bit of chatting we backtracked and ran into one of our group that had been late joining back up— Malena. She joined us on our walk instead of trying to find the others and we set off to the Pineta di Montecatini Terme, which we had only been able to read snippets about online.

The pine forest was vast and maze-like with many smaller unique sections comprising a kaleidoscope whole. We wandered past beautiful pink villas

VI

glowing warmly against the sky as it faded from cobalt to navy. Umbrella pines stood proud here as well and the great twisting forms were starkly silhouetted against the sunset.

We discovered paths running through wide open areas of field and an almost English-style hedge row. Finding ourselves on the other side and somehow a twenty minute walk from home, we had a fairly good idea of where to explore the next morning but no idea where we currently were.

Through providence alone we found the city center— bustling with activity and kids playing games across the stone square between the fountain and church well past ten o'clock.

Here the three of us became five as we ran into Emma and Catherine on the walk home. We spent time by the fountain— Italy at night is a dream waking— but eventually made it back to sleep well before the next day's mysteries could be uncovered.

Girasole— to turn toward the sun

VII

silver sage

en route to montecatini-terme, federica asks us,
jet-lagged and bleary eyed, if we know how to spot
                              the olive trees
speckled along the sloping countryside.

laura's voice emerges from the fog in answer:
they're silvery. federica is pleased, points out
                              the lovely trees
hidden amongst the thickets. *silver sage,*

she calls them. she tells us about
the olives, bellies swollen—
                              sun-ripened,
but still so bitter that you cannot

eat them straight from the branches.
you must take care to coax that
                              golden elixir
from the acrid flesh. federica's voice

floats on, weaving tapestries of histories
and flowing ever onward, identifying
                              the landmarks
spattering the tuscan countryside, but

I am still dreaming of the olive trees,
silver-veined and shimmering
                              in the sunlight.
I too wish to coax something beautiful

from all this bitterness, to extract
what's good, to create my own
                              liquid gold—
and as the trees leave me behind

the slow curve of the road,
I long to find myself amongst them,
                              silver-veined
and always reaching for the sun.

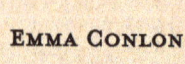
EMMA CONLON

I need to etch these hills
into my memory
because there was not a moment
to take photos
and they wouldn't do justice them anyway—
and I don't know
if I'll ever return
because days are so numbered
and minutes slip away
faster than the toll
of a cruel clock

LEIGH FISHER

45

III.

11:11, Make a wish.

Home we claim on an Umbrian cliffside. Love we make when we speak and lock eyes. A wish we say each moment this minute passes. You name me "Wildflower", one that blooms in tufa. A flower that grows in cobblestone. I name you "Star", a light that shines. A love I'm always reaching for.

11:11. Make a wish. To be wild and shine. Together. Just as this town taught us to once before.

IIIa.

Il s'appelle la fleur sauvage.
Elle s'appelle son étoile.
Comme Le Petit Prince et sa rose,
Ces deux amoureuse voyagent à nouveau

Sunflower

I've never seen
Sunflowers like this,
fields and Fields
of Sunflowers.
I don't think
I've ever seen
more than ten at a time.
And now I've seen thousands.

That's what I hope
loving you will feel like.

MELISSA DAVID

Lettera a me stesso

I packed you in a box,
Folded somewhere between
old photographs and dusty recipes
Memories of a girl, a wild sunflower
bursting with a universal glow
Back when primitive nature
had a sense of wonder,
Its silent song carries
the weight of ancient grain,
The synchronicities of life
where soul meets matter
I'll go back to that box from time to time,
to remind me what it is like to be truly alive
I'll think fondly of that girl
who once basked in that universal light,
Even though I may not feel you as much as I'd like,
Your silent song will always whisper softly
the constant nature of a flower went wild

Letter to myself

DENAE TERESE

Worse are the words not spoke than those said amiss

To live without love is to die without living

Poetry is meant to describe

that which cannot be explained

J.S.

Hotel

MELISSA DAVID

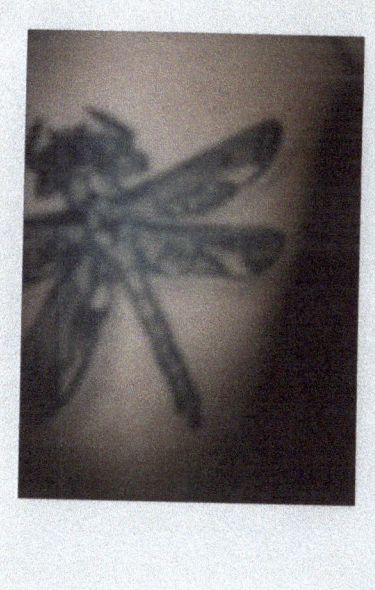

MELISSA DAVID

123

Ona dueva tre
I attempt in terrible Italian.
Anneta behind the counter giggles, correcting me,
As she hands me the weighted key from the sands of time.

123
I grasp the key suddenly not able to breathe
As I slide into the communist size elevator.

123
I trace the numbers
Slowly suffocating from the lack of air circulation.

123
Finally I'm released from 1974
And step into *The Shinning*,
Half expecting Jack Nicholson to pop out
Of the red door at the end of the hallway.

1...2...3
I start to sing, she snaps her head to the right,
Really? She says, staring straight at me,
Attempting to roll her eyes.

1...2...3
She says with assurance
Between attempted breaths.
No other words left, just

123
I hold her hand and tell her
I love her
She looks at me
And tells me she loves me too.
She knows it's the last time,
I know it's the last time.

MELISSA DAVID

123

I sit in the empty room
With what's left of her.
I whisper *goodbye mom,*
Hoping death is still in the room
And will carry my message,
To the other side.

123

The silence is broken
by the doctors outside
Waiting for directions.
I take a deep breath and think

123

I awake from the daydream,
Standing, dripping sweat
In front of my tuscan red door.
The warm tears mix down my chest.
I take a deep breath and open my door
NUMBER 123

MELISSA DAVID

Montecatini Terme - Tuscany

printed in Italy

Montecatini is renowned for its natural thermal springs, the beneficial waters sourced from an aquifer fed by waters infused with minerals from the Triassic period.

A UNESCO World Heritage Site - the town exemplifies the living histories of spa resort towns that were incredibly popular from the 18th- 20th centuries.

Edizioni D'Arte I.F.I. Firenze
Riproduzione vietata

Intro Workshop

Catherine's Notes
from class
→

- Pay attention to the world around you because you see things that no one else sees.

- Don't be perfect. Be raw, honest, and real. "Anything honest is worthwhile." - R. Clift

- Your art is worthy now. You don't have to wait for permission from another.

- Respect what is written. It's a piece of your soul on paper. So, don't belittle it.

- Inspiration can't be controlled. Let it happen. Find poetry in the mundane.

- Everything is poetry

- More specificity, more connection

- If you can learn to not judge upon meeting something or someone, you might be able to know them for who they are

- Don't give up on your art because it will not fail you.

Exquisite Corpse Poems

i wish people could see the way you are (KC)
your comfort, your light, your memory

you could be anywhere you want,

(LF) whether your body moves an inch
or a thousand miles across the world
it's all a matter of what's in your head
Reflects the way you see the world
Feed into what you would like to see (OH)
Learn all that you could be

Stretch into the deepest depths of yourself

walk every street, ~~eve~~ meet every person

hear every story, breath all of it in

(LF) inhale all the voices, warnings, and stories
exhale it all into a tale of your own

and release your voice into the world
Because without it where would we be
but an empty space of something sweet (OH)
~~the what~~ one can have in a single heartbeat
The affect

could change every perspective you

thought you had, tipping and

reshaping the world view as it fits you.

Kaitlyn, Leigh, Denae

C.RenéP.   I choose to believe in her
           in you, and in me.
           What alternative
Jenni Lucci   is the choice to love
           or the choice to be loved?

           She asked

Mel   Do you mind if I smoke now?
           as the Italian wind blows her red dress

           Her lips matching.
           Her cadence reveals her soul
           and she's learning to generously share.
C.RenéP.   Her eyes twinkle as her pen glides on the paper,
           I loved watching her with stars in
                                    her eyes

Jenni Lucci   even on an overcast night
           Her light shined like the
                           eifel tower
           When I think of her now I smile
Mel   forever frozen in time she laughs

           I wish my children knew her now.
           Oh, how they would be so proud
           to know her blood runs through their veins.
C.RenéP.   Her legacy doesn't need to be world renoun.
           All that matters, is that it has been
           passed down.

Catherine, Jen, Mel

I am haunted by ghosts everywhere I am

I see them in scents and hear them in sights

I know not who they are only that we have not met

I hear whispers of a laugh I wish I know well

A coffee order to remember ~ Laura

A story yet to be told

waiting on a dusty shelf,
worn pages peeking out between leather ends,
well loved by souls who will never hold them again. ~ Freydis

Only to wonder if they themselves were

even loved in the first place to begin with

So here I stand asking can I be loved if I do not love

Can I reach for you if my hands are shaking

If my voice is not worthy

Would you hear me if I called your name
or would my words pass by in silence like the wind—
always escaping your ear, your heart?
A summer day fades to fall, darling, and I—
I am already falling with the leaves.

J.S., Laura, & Freydis

I came to Italy to finish writing
the words that have
been stuck in my throat for 3 long years.
those unspoken words whose echoes
linger still within my chest ee

I clutch to breathe, perhaps cry hoping to see.

It's a voice that calls me home and brightens the whole
world.

Your silent voice travels across the room; I know
You love me too.
                                                    -CM

I keep ~~that~~ knowledge ~~a~~ like ~~treasures~~ in my heart

Take it out when I need a little extra to get
me through

when my legs feel stuck, ~~and I you hope you~~
~~my~~ you're the one who keeps me moving
                                                    -MG

by:
Emma Conlon
Cas McDowell
Malena Grace

To write an exquisite corpse poem, each
participant takes turns writing on a sheet of
paper, folding it to conceal all but their last
verse, and then passing it to the next poet.
keep writing until it feels done— trust in
your intuition & trust in your words.
                                                    - R.

Emma, Cas, Malena

"You're like this little Italian model that Italia has missed."
- Jenni G.

"If I have acne and gray hair at the same time I'm going to lose it."
- Emma W.

"I don't know why I recorded it, but I thank God that I did."
- Kaitlyn

"Your poetry is like music."
- Rachel

"Your cadence is so beautiful."
- Kaitlyn

07/04/22

The Artist's SuperMarket

To share your art
is to share your produce.
It's the seeds
to someone else's inspiration.
What you offer might just be the key
to unlock their mind or heart.
But, if you keep it to yourself
your produce might never grow.
Or, maybe it will just feed your soul
when it could have fed the whole world.

CATHERINE PITTS

Twins

Twins are super connected,
The tales are true.
I watch them bounce off each other,
Never tiring of each-others company.
Their souls have been intertwined
Since the last century.
When one cries,
I feel the other start to well up
On the other side
Of the room.
Must be strange,
Having half of you,
Outside your body,
Inescapably connected.

MELISSA DAVID

She cries like the sun -
iridescent rays streaking golden cheeks,
and I wonder if she knows
just how beautiful she is, here,
breaking through shadows
and harnessing the happiness
so many of us have forgotten.

We have been told for too long
that you can only cry when you're sad,
or upset, or angry.

She is reminding the world
that joy is also a flood.

FREYDIS LOVA

I once lived a life so guarded off
I didn't know
where the ramparts ended
and where my heart began

but I've broken free
of every prison cell
that has ever tried
to hold me

now I wander beyond
these castle walls
no longer held back
by the tower's ghost
who goes by your name

Rampart Heart
ram·part
/'ram,pärt/

the defensive wall of a castle or walled city,
having a broad top with a walkway and typically a
stone parapet.
"a castle with ramparts and a moat"
"the defense around a closed heart"

heart
/härt/

a hollow organ in the center of the chest
that pumps blood through the body in the manner of
rhythmic contraction and dilation.
"she reached for her heart and winced"
"the fickle thing whose biggest enemy is the reason of the mind"

LEIGH FISHER

CINTA SAYA KEPADAMU
BUKAN SENANG DILIHATI,
KAMI HANYA MAMPU,
MEMANDANG SESAMA DIRI.

DENGAN BULAN GEMILANG
SEBAGAI SAKSI,
AKANKU MEMEGANG INGATAN
YANG DICIPTA OLEH KITA BERDUA.

BIARLAH BISIKAN ANGIN
YANG LEMBUT,
MEMBAWA NOTA CINTAKU PADAMU.

BILA KAU MENDENGAR
RAHSIA DALAM HATIKU,
INGATLAH BAHAWA
SAYA YANG MASIH MENUNGGU
KETIBAAN MU,
CINTAKU.

MY LOVE FOR YOU
IS NOT SO EASILY SEEN,
WE COULD ONLY AFFORD,
TO STEAL GLANCES AT ONE ANOTHER.

WITH THE MOON
AS OUR WITNESS,
I WILL HOLD THE MEMORIES,
THAT WE HAVE CREATED TOGETHER.

THE WHISPER OF THE WIND
WILL BRING TO YOU
THE NOTES OF MY LOVE FOR YOU.

WHEN YOU HEAR
THE SECRETS OF MY HEART,
REMEMBER THAT I AM WAITING FOR YOU,
MY LOVE.

KAITLYN YÍNG YUÉ

IV.

Bach, Beethoven and Mozart too.
Vivaldi, Tchaikovsky.
Can you give me something new?
Light fingers on heavy keys,
You wrote in a way
They never moved too aimlessly.
An opera, a ballet, and a symphony -
Trap my mind in colour.
A glow of synthesis, your notes are peace.
Sometimes anger. But most of all
They give a safe place to think.

Please keep playing.
My heart will follow in tune.
Thank you for giving these
Songs for us to play, hum, and dance.
Even when we are unsure if
The piece is actually you.

CAS MCDOWELL

70

Artist Hive Mind

I've been watching that lizard,
"Me too!!!"
I knock on wood
"Me too!!!"
I save little things for my memoirs
"Me too!!"

I walk in random bookstores
and see you there too.
The likeness of the artist
has made our souls shine through.
To view the world through this lens
is a culture of its own,
it's beautiful and broken
and a gift to this world,
especially when we aren't alone.

CATHERINE PITTS

71

With Beauty comes Death

Disease always creeps into the beauty,
Lying underneath.

With Beauty comes Death.

It is next to me, but I don't mind.
I'm used to keeping it company.
I touch it, Knowing it's on my fingertips.

Others deny it,
As it slowly takes them over.
It's here.
It's always here.
Spreading through the air,
Feeding on the art,
That was once our beauty.

Solarium

A Southern Man
Sits in the garden veranda
His light vest,
Sits over his summer shirt,
As his tattoo peaks through his sleeves.
Tailored brown shoes sit
By his matching tailored
Brown satchel
He is happy here
He is himself.

Catherine

Can I touch her hair?
Are we there?
I've been by myself for so long,
I'm not sure if I can touch her hair.
She looks over and whispers,
We're there.

MELISSA DAVID

MELISSA DAVID

73

Verde

I never knew color could have a smell,
but when I immerse myself in nature
and breathe in deeply of its silent freedom,
The scent of the trees will
always bring me back to the color green

Green

– Denae Terese

Montecatini Terme - Basilica di S. Maria Assunta

a fortuitous meeting

we amble through this place
with all the exhilaration of
small children in a toy store.
we glow with the streetlamps.

we are lit from within.

in the square, by the fountain,
we bump into three familiar
strangers. three strangers
we will soon call soulmates.

we talk by the fountain
for over an hour—trade secrets,
share hopes & dreams & all
matter of beautiful things.

tomorrow, we will travel together.
a few days from now, we will
write poems about each other.
less than a week from now,

we will say goodbye.

today, we are five strangers
electrified with the ecstasy
of happenstance, the precious
joy of being alive.

EMMA CONLON

Drink with me in a setting sun parlor
and together, let's give life to an exquisite corpse.
Let's take turns stringing words together
through smoke and dust, sharing our heartbreak
and woes, line by line, never truly knowing
what the other means until we are out of breath,
or ink, or paper. Let's see how our hearts
bleed poetry born from abandonment and longing,
of love, and lust, and life, and every messy moment
in between. Let's fall, fold by fold, and rediscover
ourselves in the darkness that is soon to come.

Only then will our eyes be illuminated
by what we have forgotten to say.

Only then will we discover how well our souls fit together.

FREYDIS LOVA

when souls of the same star family

meet in this human lifetime

it's a remembrance of a truth meant to be shared

they are loved ones you may have just met -

yet, your spirits have danced through the cosmos

for lifetimes together

and to hear them tell their stories

since the last time you waltzed through the galaxies -

brings you back home to your human heart

JENNIFER GELLOCK

Roman Cousin

I still remember the warm Tuscan summers at your mother's estate.
Sent away from Rome each summer, I'd find you deep in the dark library,
Buried in a book only made for ten people, and you,
a ten-year-old viscount in the making.

10 years younger than your oldest sibling.
You spent most of your life walking the halls of this villa alone,
Making friends with the ghosts,
Until the first day of summer,
When your roman cousin trots in on the city coach.

I still remember the sunflowers,
The buzz of the summer bugs,
Silently exploring searching for prehistoric bones.
We found bones once.
We kept them in a secret place, only known by us.
We use to spend hours exploring your cold granite house,
Playing hide and seek.
The only sound, the little pitter-patter of our feet.
As we got older we would just sit and read,
Under our grandmother's willow tree.

I remember those summers fondly,
They made this city girl complete.
It was a place of peace for me.
You, my country cousin,
In my Tuscan retreat.

MELISSA DAVID

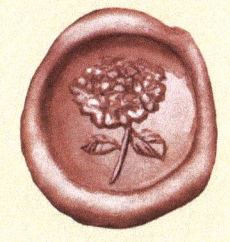

4th july, 2022

we've arrived in Tuscany! the bus ride here was fun, i've always had good memories associated with travelling by buses. just pretty landscapes and music for a few hours. tuscany feels like such a charming place already, i can tell i'm going to really like it here.

‡‡‡

so rachel's introductory workshop had ended just minutes earlier, and i'm... speechless. in a good way. there's so much to process, really, even though it was casual enough. to have heard her personal story of how she started writing and her own inspirations, i almost cried. i don't know all the stories of the people here just yet, but i know we're each carrying something profound. i honestly don't know what the days will bring.

KAITLYN YÍNG YUÉ

July 5th

Montecatini Terme
&
Castello del Trebbio

Nothing short of magic. Today, I was hoping to find the perfect outdoor classroom— and it found us. I taught a workshop on inspiration in an ancient Terme— like a Roman bath. These towering ivory marble pillars surrounded us, a calm crystal blue pool, soft music, hidden passageways and secrets around each corner. I encouraged my poets to try a new medium— I handed out film cameras and watercolor supplies and dip pens and sketching pencils and to my absolute joy— they embraced them wholeheartedly. I released them in to the beautiful space and some went off on their own, some together, but they all were on a mission to create. It was astonishing to witness.

It was as if we were tapping into an ancient energy of old— one that connected us through simply the desire to create. For the next several hours— they were like fountains— writing, painting, drawing, reading alout to each other, eating peaches, dancing, singing— it was as if I was observing magical creatures, like nymphs, in their most natural form. It's amazing what happens when you tell an artist they are good enough, they are worthy, then give them space to soak in inspiration and create. I buzzed arouns like a bee, checking in on each of them individually. I love getting to know them— I think I've gathered eleven of the most incredible people on this earth.

We made our way to a castle in Tuscany, the tour was fascinating. I trailed behind all my poets, gazing at them and the expressions on their faces more than the historical marvels around me. I still have a hard time believing, standing in this dim wine cellar while a man named Sieno tells us about the aging process— that they all chose to fly to Italy with me. Me.?! It's almost impossible to fathom— so I'll just have to settle for being overwhelmingly grateful. To end the night, we stumbled upon a symphony and danced in the shadows of a magnificent garden. This day was right out of a fairytale.

R. CLIFT

July 5

On this morning our breakfast corner was established. The dining room was large with two levels and felt like a slight jump back in time like most of the hotel. White cloth covered the round tables decorated with glassware and cutlery. An assortment of foods were strewn about the room almost randomly- by the front door were the savories- eggs and salamis and breads. Across the first sitting area and up the few stairs was fruit, coffee, and around the corner hid the pastries.

All of the mugs available were older than I was and emblazoned with faded logos reading HTP on the outside. Of course, these were espresso cups and little tea cups, rather than the large diner mugs we're used to back home. A machine nearby gurgled out a surprisingly tasty array of cappuccinos, ciccolatos, and americanos.

We staked out a larger table out of the way. The windows behind us were tall, and surrounded by the orange and blue striped walls, it felt a little like we were stuck somewhere between a 1920s Ritz and big top circus.

We ate and chattered and an old tendency of mine cropped up as we left. I'd taken extra bread from the table and a few slices of salami and made a simple little sandwich to wrap up in a napkin for later.

"Once a backpacker," I suppose. A traveler noticed and I shrugged—

"I love hotel breakfasts, they can last to lunch too, if you think ahead."

It wasn't terribly uncommon for someone to have squirreled away an orange or a roll in the coming days after that occurrence.

Meeting by the piano in the lobby, a few of the travelers were playing songs they'd learned long ago on the contrasting keys. The sound was as faded and out of tune as memories. Once we were all gathered, we walked together through Montecatini to the park.

We kept to the path we'd discovered the night before— everything was much easier to see and identify now in the light. Small buildings appeared that had seemed gigantic before. Neighborhoods stretched far where they had been lost in shadow. Like first arriving in a garden at night only to discover swaths of new flowers in the morning.

Eventually, we strolled up to the multicolored glass and iron entrance of the Terme Tettucio, a drinking spa. The entire Terme was enormous— with sentinels of stone, pale blue fountains, painted ceilings, and glasswork above. Sun-

VIII

light shining in was golden and sage green and vermillion. We moved through the enchanted space with the steady pace of a cathedral visitor.

The other guests who were at the Terme to find comfort or healing in the waters sat in the center courtyard with glass and silver cups. Along the far wall was a series of taps flowing with waters with different meanings. Great mosaics depicted the purpose from curing diabetes to helping with aging to aiding fertility. We were told emphatically that we could not drink the water without first visiting a doctor— so we just admired and wondered.

Rachel found a grove of trees in the park surrounding the complex for our next workshop. Her topic centered around inspiration, and it's various forms.

Then— we were all set free to explore and create. Many travelers found a tree or bench or table to sit at and write. A few of us stayed together at a stone building near the back of the park where Rachel demonstrated dip pens and ink and I gave tips on using watercolors.

We painted together and read poems aloud and braided each other's hair. Like an old painting of mythic figures lazing about in a flourishing garden, calling upon the muses, we spent away the afternoon.

When it was time to go it was difficult to wake and leave the dream behind. So much so, that we were a bit late but beaming once we made it to the awaiting bus for our next adventure. After another scenic drive through Tuscany we arrived at an old castle in the center of a valley of vineyards called Castello del Trebbio.

It belonged to the Pazzi family— who, it seemed, behaved so badly in Florentine history that they were all banished and the castle stood empty for 400 years. Eventually, however, someone came along and decided it could be of some use.

During the derelict age the land did not go to waste. It continued to be cultivated by the families nearby and they went on to create celebrated olive oil and wine that is still in production today. We started with our guide, Simone, who related all of this history to us as we toured through the castle and the winery within.

This structure was a proper castle, you must understand. It was the kind read about in fairytales. Every room was ancient and echoing and melancholic and wonderful.

We eventually made our way through the maze of the winery (in what may have been a dungeon before) to the castle courtyard bedecked with garlands

IX

of blooms and overflowing pots of flowers as if decorated for a festival. It was the last cheerful heartbeat of the old place— complete with a wishing well in the center and a view of the sunny Tuscan hills beyond the metal gate.

It was to the right of this happy space where the kitchen resided and where we met Jerry— the chef who would teach us to make pasta from scratch. He was jolly and exact and a truly wonderful teacher. We donned aprons and went through each step from cracking eggs into wells of flour to making two sauces over the stove. A few volunteers went up at a time to not overcrowd the cooking and gave the rest of us a chance to cheer them on as they rolled pasta dough to impossibly large, thin circles under Jerry's guidance.

Once everything was prepared we moved to the opposite side of the court-yard where the old dining hall still stood proud. The ceilings were impossibly high and an old iron ring was set at the very top center where I imagine a chande-lier once swayed. We were greeted with plates of bread, meats, and cheeses and Simone explained a few of their best wines as we tasted them.

They have a "house wine" (and I particularly like this story) that they made to turn the definition of house wine around. Usually the type is the cheap-est available, but at Castello del Trebbio— it's their best. They don't sell it. They only share it with those who visit, who are guests in their home. It was truly lovely.

Our pasta arrived on platters— veggie cream and wild boar ragu. The noodles were of varying widths and a little wild, but they were both fantastic. We even got Federica's surprised approval.

The acoustics of the hall were so tempting that two of our travelers sang. Mel and Emma chose songs and sang for us and even the castle staff stopped to listen. Bright evening light cut in from the narrow window behind like a spot-light. It was magic.

We caught the sun setting over the Tuscan hills as we walked back the short path to the bus. We may see the sun every day— but I'm convinced golden hour was created for Italy alone.

The piano in the lobby became our regular meeting spot and after a moment of rest we went out for an evening walk. We meandered past families and even befriended a very happy dog named Bruno who insisted on chatting with everyone he saw despite his owner's wishes.

We passed by the Terme again only to discover an orchestra playing inside. They were local students of music and it was free to enter, so we did and donated a few euros each anyway. The sound ringing through the stone arches

x

was magnificent. Grandparents and cousins sat in rows before the assembled musicians taking photos on phones and tablets. Kaitlyn was especially excited because she loved classical music but had never seen it live. I was happy to believe this moment was put before our path just for her.

Our little group stood in the back under the painted dome ceiling— but when they began to play *Once Upon a Dream* I turned to Freydis (we had bonded over fairytales before) and said,

"Will you dance with me?"

Without hesitation she smiled and said "Yes." And we discreetly ran to the back of the park under deep shadow and far enough away not to be seen. We laughed when we noticed Cas, Rachel, and J.S., had followed instantly and we all frollicked about and spun eachother under the cascade of music until we ran short of breath and fell back into the dewy grass. The song dissolved into the stars and we walked steadily and quietly back— quite pleased to not have attracted a single person's attention during our escapade.

Once the sweeping music was over, we turned in with the echoes of the day still playing through our dreams.

XI

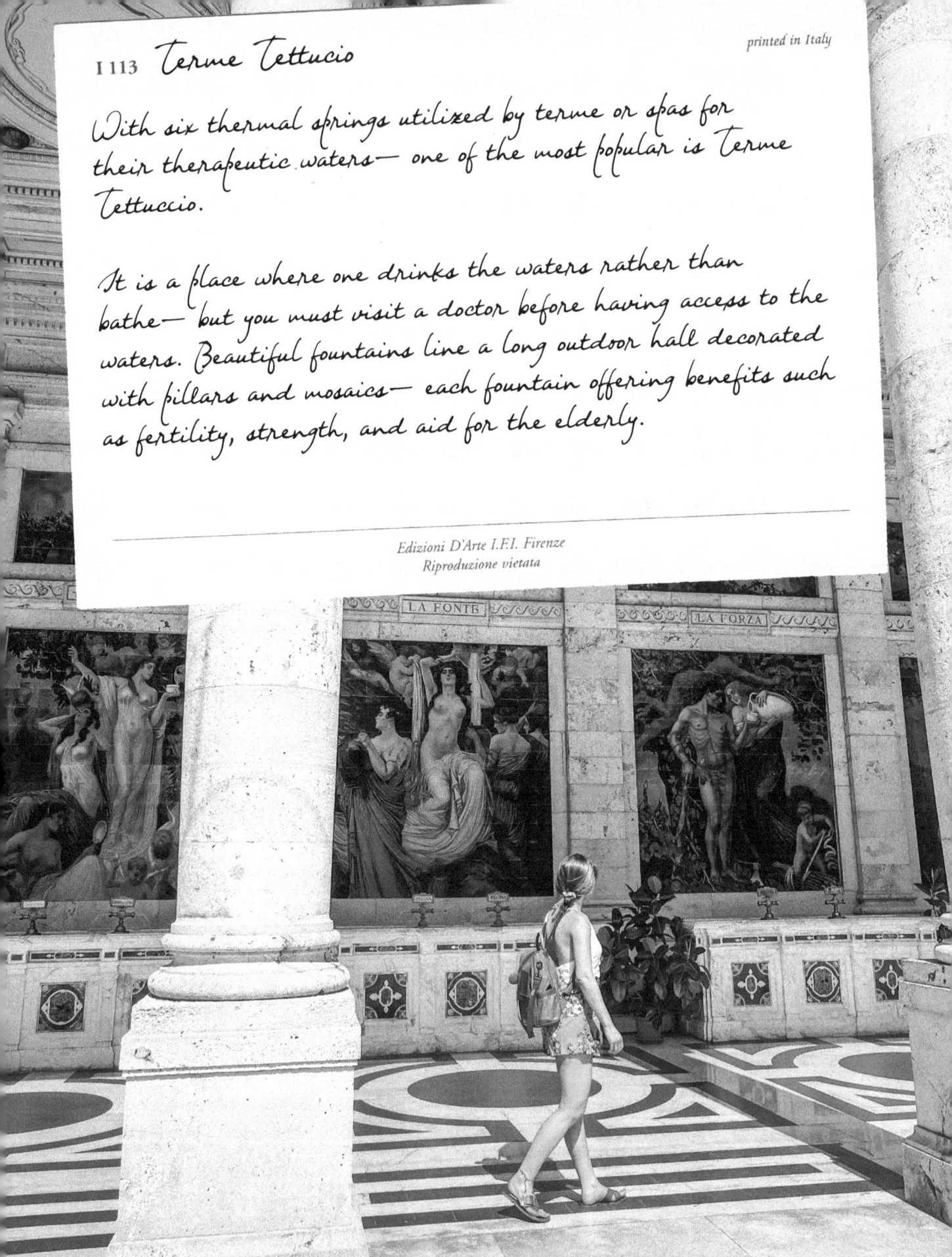

I 113 *Terme Tettucio*

With six thermal springs utilized by terme or spas for their therapeutic waters— one of the most popular is Terme Tettuccio.

It is a place where one drinks the waters rather than bathe— but you must visit a doctor before having access to the waters. Beautiful fountains line a long outdoor hall decorated with pillars and mosaics— each fountain offering benefits such as fertility, strength, and aid for the elderly.

Edizioni D'Arte I.F.I. Firenze
Riproduzione vietata

Art & Poetry Workshop One

sono un POETA

I am a poet - in Italian

An Excerpt from
Catherine's Journal

ode to an ornamental flower on the ceiling of café storico

at first glance, you may seem slight and unassuming.
you do not draw attention to yourself. their eyes
slip over you without registering your presence.
delicate as you are, you prefer your place among
the shadows in spite of the strength bestowed upon
you by the marble from whose head you sprang forth
from, guided into being by time-worn, patient hands.
you may not entrance the ordinary passersby or
attract attention like the scalloped centerpiece, a frozen
scroll trapped in a moment, wind-purled and enduring.
you are a shier creature, a rarer beast. content to tuck
away amongst your ornate siblings, assured in your
supporting role. shun the spotlight if you must,
but I hope you do not underestimate your worth.
you are unnoticed, alabaster and streaked with fawny
taupe against the pale buttermilk of the crumbling
frescoed ceiling, so ordinary and so remarkably rare.
you are beguiling in your own distinctive quiet way.
forgive me, fiore, for singing your praises, for admiring
your demure florescence, for not noticing you sooner
crouching in wait, holding your breath for a new day.

EMMA CONLON

These photos were taken on a film camera and developed months later!

— Jen

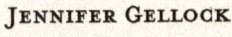

JENNIFER GELLOCK

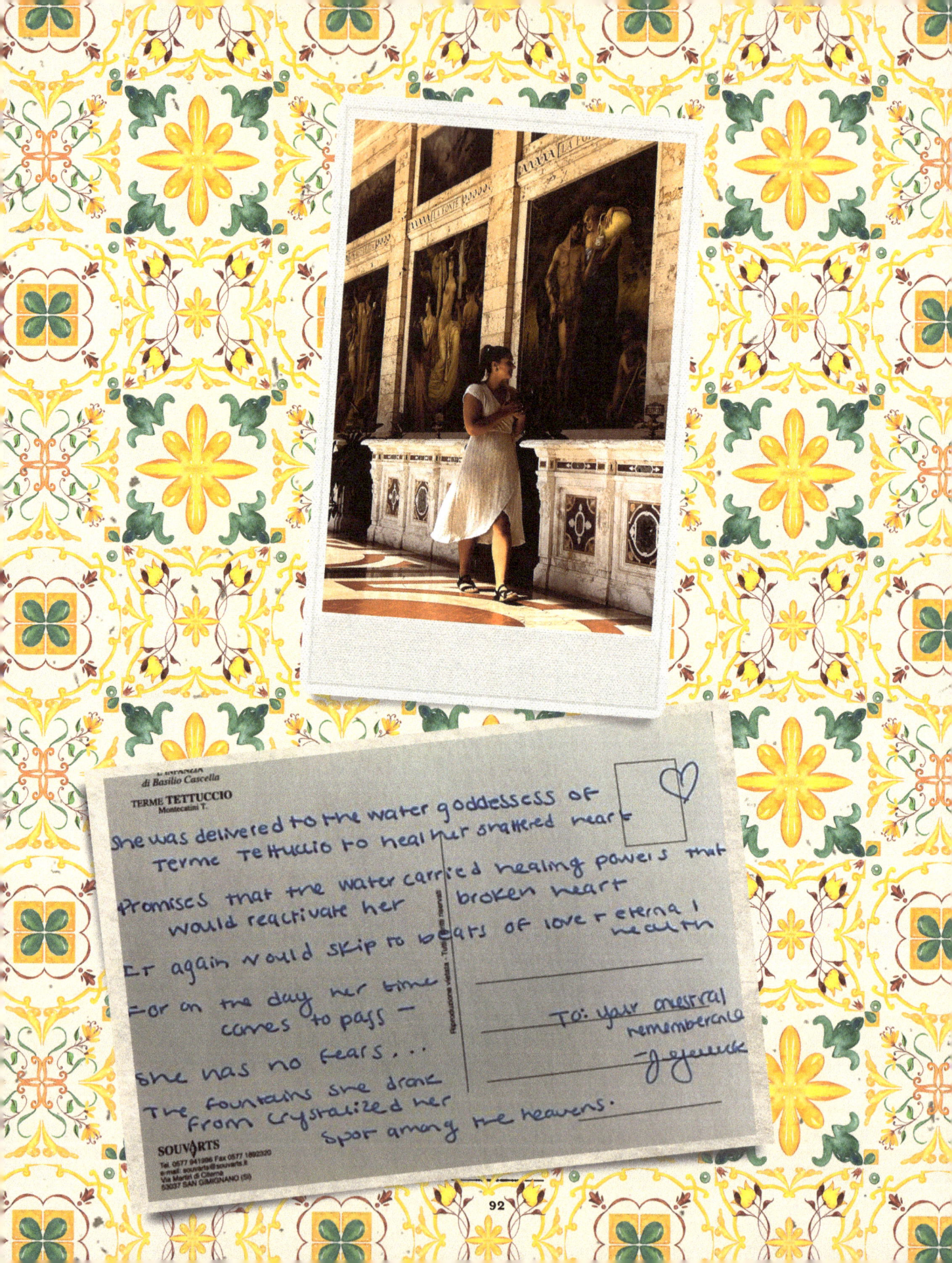

She was delivered to the water goddessess of
   Terme Tettuccio to heal her shattered heart

promises that the water carried healing powers that
      would reactivate her   broken heart

It again would skip to beats of love & eternal
                                        health

For on the day her time
    comes to pass —

she has no fears...
   The fountains she drank
      from crystalized her
          spot among the heavens.

To: your ancestral
      remembrance
      — J Jennette

She was delivered to the water goddesses
of Terme Tettuccio
to heal her shattered heart
Promises that the water carried healing powers
that would reactivate her heart

It again would skip to beats of love and eternal health
For on the day her time comes to pass –
She knows her spirit was once renewed
by the ancient waters of the Earth

So she has no fears

The fountains she drank from
crystalized her spot among the heavens

JENNIFER GELLOCK

THERE ARE GODDESSES IN THE GARDEN.

HEAR THEIR LAUGHTER THROUGH THE OLIVE TREES,
ON THE STREAMS OF SUNLIGHT,
AND THE SOFT WINDS,
AND IN THE LAST FEW DROPS OF DEW
THAT ADORN THE IVY LIKE DIAMONDS
AND SAPPHIRES AND EMERALDS.

WALK UP THE HIDDEN STEPS
GROWN OUT OF ROOTS AND BROKEN STATUES
AND FIND THEM
ON THE EDGE OF MARBLE,
WEAVING WISHES INTO THE DAY,
SINGING SOFTLY,
HARMONIZING WHEN THE SHADOWS COME,
DANCING WHEN THE AMBER SKY
BREAKS THROUGH RUNES.

THEY PAINT THE WORLD AS IT IS
IN THAT MOMENT. RAINBOW AND SEPIA,
FILTERED THROUGH HURT AND LOVE.
THEY ALL SEE THE WORLD DIFFERENTLY,
AND YET, THEIR SMILES ALL FALL THE SAME
ON SOFT LIPS AND IN FORGOTTEN DREAMS—
BE THEM FROM THE ELDERLY WOMAN
WHO PASSES BY AND HEARS A LINE
THAT BRINGS HER BACK TO HER CHILDHOOD,
OR A LITTLE GIRL WHO STOPS TO WATCH
HAIR BEING BRAIDED BETWEEN GOLDEN BEADS,
OR THE COUPLE— YOUNG AND IN LOVE—
WHO DON'T UNDERSTAND A WORD
THESE WOMEN ARE SPEAKING.

TO EVERY SOUL THAT FEELS
THE SLIGHTEST BIT LOST:

THERE ARE GODDESSES IN THE GARDEN—
AND THEY ARE WAITING TO WELCOME YOU.

FREYDIS LOVA

There are
goddesses
in the
garden.

-freydis lova

Braids

I've met her.
My future child.
I straighten her royal blue silk corset
And slide her long braided hair our of her face
Behind her plastic elvin ears.
Her green eyes from another century smile at me.
I take her freckled hand
As we walk to the archery stand.
Other children are screaming and fumbling
with their bows.
They all stop and turn as her arrow pierces
the centre of the target.
She turns and lifts her chin at me,
As she has just singled the beginning of a battle.
I am so happy she has chosen me
To be her mother in this lifetime
My little warrior princess.

MELISSA DAVID

A Love Letter to Inward Athlete

You were the first thing
I never rushed

We took our time
I breathed you in slowly
carried you
around with me
as I listened
to how you wanted
to tell your story

I held you softly

Cradled you
with only the purest
of intentions
you were my muse for years

Conversations between us
never went stale

I can hear your voice still

Wafting down the halls
on repeat
in my memory

I loved you mercifully

As I wore you
clasped inside a locket
clutched tightly
to my chest

I was the musician
and you were the violin
pulling the bow slowly
across all four of your strings

Our music carried
across the Tuscan Valley together
through the marble buildings
echoing for miles
it was the longest-shortest time
I can ever remember

One day
you asked me to stay
so I let you

I never would have told you
that you were overstaying
your welcome

I still can't tell
if you were my quickest hello
or my longest goodbye

When I think back on us
you remind me of the solstice

The longest day
in the heat of the summer

Sometimes we would drive all night
just to watch the sunrise together
and as the light would begin to shine
on a brand new day
we'd take the longest inhale
and then we would hold our breath
to make a wish

I have to admit
after I met you
I was afraid
to let go
and exhale again

JENNIFER GELLOCK

What if I never knew
another like you?

What if wishes never came true
the same way again?

Yet, deep down
I always had a knowing
that one day
you would get swept away
with the tides
and that makes sense to me
because the ocean
was our favorite place
to spend the day

So I sent you off
as a message in a bottle
just as the high tide
rolled in

And I watched with tears
in my eyes
as you drifted out to sea
and got picked up
in the waves

I bid you farewell
then got on my knees
and thanked the sand

For letting us daydream upon her
during all those summers
when we were together
You let the stars
be your guide
sailing across the ocean
at night
as you made your way

to a new destination

As you washed upon
the coastline
I prayed you would land
into the hands
of new loving strangers

Ones who deeply yearned for guidance
to walk a sovereign path together

For in my message
inside your bottle
all I left was my contact

Then like magic
you brought me my people

You changed my life
and I'll never forget you

[Note: This poem is a love letter to my
business Inward Athlete. I wrote it in a stream
of consciousness watching an Italian middle
school orchestra play at the Terme Tettuccio
on a magical night under the stars. As the
music played, I sat there and dreamed about
sending my new business, Inward Athlete,
out into the world.]

JENNIFER GELLOCK

07/05/22

Beautiful Soul

Your soul is so beautiful,
I feel a call to respond to it.
You inspire my thoughts and my art.

Not because you asked,
but because you are.

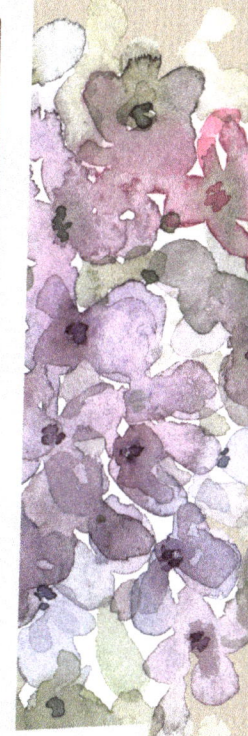

CATHERINE PITTS

101

It's been at least a decade
since I've used watercolors.
When I was in school,
I was always told I was using them wrong.

I never understood that.
I mixed the paint with water—

what could I be doing wrong?

I pick up a brush from the unrolled holder
and I hear their voices.
Former art teachers start to lecture me,
telling me that my piece looks too vibrant,
or too muted, or too unfamiliar.

I cover a page in my journal with warm water
and let the corners roll, saturated in "what ifs."

I feel the brush being yanked from my hand.
I see my paper being taken off the table.
I realize my eyes are closed.
I open them.
My journal is in my lap.
The brush is cradled between my fingers.
The only voices I hear are those of the ones who care.

I make the first stroke with orange.
If no one will teach me—
if they will only take my work
and turn it into what they want—
then I will teach myself.

I will paint with water, and pigments,
and joy, and pain, and when I am done,
every word they threw at me that tarnished
my creativity will be left among the runes,
turned into something beautiful by being
dipped in the springs and healed with my hands.

FREYDIS LOVA

Stagioni di me

With every inner storm
lies a rainbow just beyond the shore,
I wonder if its wreckage looks the same
from afar as it does to me near,
How tides give the illusion of chaos
only to find a silver-lining beating at its core
Shimmering sustenance
in every heartbeat within in reason,
I wonder if you will continue
to love me as I weather my own seasons,
A change in the air
gives rise to native emotion,
How a newborn perspective
can alter the course of our discretion
The dance between you and I
are similar but much distinct,
No storm the same
in the changing of each season,
From core to color
we evolve in different light,
Tell me there is an antidote
to carry us within reason
Is it beauty in the contrast
as we go through transformation?
The constant in our hearts
as we weather every condition
Like a rainbow holding
the hands of a swept up shore,
I'll take yours if you'll take mine
through every breakthrough
world we explore

Seasons of Me

DENAE TERESE
———

Adam Could Have Said No

They say she seduced him
That her feminine powers were no match to his manly consciousness
Or his will to decline her offerings
So they martyred her with humanity's downfall
They threw the Bible at her
And then all men began to rise from her rubbles
A patriarchal upheaval
How could she be solely to blame for humankind's exile?
You see -
There's always been a missing piece to this scriptured-puzzle
He always had a choice -
Adam could have said no

JENNIFER GELLOCK

[Note: A response to R. Clift's Ekphrastic poem titled, "Even is Shown Recoiling" Inspired by a sculpture of Eve, 1883 by Auguste Rodin]

To me a true friend is as rare

as a true love

An artist should never seek help
to create what is already inside of them,
rather they should
seek inspiration instead

J.S.

To have the perfect words only after the moment has passed

is the best way I can describe a curse

J.S.

sono un poeta

eight years ago, I wrote in this same notebook
an old Picasso line: *art is a lie that reveals truth,*
surely a butchered misquote from a complicated
person (though who among us isn't), a quote
I scribbled down for an assignment in which
I needed to evaluate and respond to his claim.
this is all to say words have a way of finding you
at the very moment you find yourself needing them.

under the shade of an umbrella tree, a constellation
poet bids us to repeat her words to ourselves.
　　　　　　　　　sono un poeta.
the dream we hadn't dared speak. the tender
counsel we had yearned for. the gentle reminder
that even in the midst of my long winters,
spring calls from beyond the bend of the river,
　　　　　　　　　thawing still.

EMMA CONLON

―――――――

FREYDIS LOVA

We're candids.
nothing posed, nothing polished or precise.
We're a mess of frizzy hair
and running makeup
and sweaty bodies
piled together in a heap of hope.

How beautiful we are,
in our most vulnerable moments.

FREYDIS LOVA

Oberon's Daydreams

I've always fantasized about
going to incredible places
where stories were spun to match
and legends once unfolded

yet even as I walk through them
with my own two feet
it still feels like a fairy tale
to see them with my own eyes

when your world starts out
so small, so limited
you forget just how large
the world really is

and I'm just waiting to be shaken
out of this reverie
by cruel fairy hands
dragging me back to reality

LEIGH FISHER

110

V.

Who will I be when I return?
Will I be the woman you
Met when we first travelled
Across the sea?
Will I be a version that pain
And hurt find the cracks to seep?
Or am I a girl whose wounds
Are wrapped in gold?
A familiar face with a new
Admiration for the difficult times.
A woman you'll welcome
Beaming and proud to hold.

CAS MCDOWELL

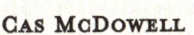

sono un poeta.
my tongue wrapped itself
around its syllables,
before my soul knew
the meaning it carried.
before knowing the home
it would carve
into my tree of life.

i never thought
i was the person who
was worth a name
to the words
that were tucked in
safely in her heart.
what more could i be,
than just a mere being
who hoped that her words
were enough to carry
the grief she felt?

i ran and danced circles
around it for years,
never daring to think
i am worthy enough to
make a home within it for myself.

but now that i have
spoken it,
and my soul knows that
this is what it means to carry it,
i never want to call myself anything else but.

sono un poeta,
i am a poet.

KAITLYN YÍNG YUÉ

112

"The beauty of being human is to experience the dark and the beautiful things and walk the line in between."

"you can do it, even if you're shaking."
— R. Clift

"imperfect, every single time... and that's what makes it beautiful."

Rachel is one who has learned to be brave and believe in her own dreams. She now leads others by the hand to do the same thing.

a page from Catherine's journal

JENNIFER GELLOCK

Take up space

"Don't take up space."
"Don't walk your pace."
"Don't be that way."

It's never as clear as that though.
Always with an undertone,
a half hazarded breath…
a certain look.

When I truly laugh someone always says,
"shhhhh."
But last time I checked…
laughter wasn't a defect.

Let me be me and do my thing.
I'll be respectful within my means.
I just will not give up being me.

CATHERINE PITTS
————

115

VII. Guardian

Master of the night,
who refuses to take flight,
sits atop my window
guarding my dreams
from the darkest frights.

Carved in stone
he permanently remains.
A grimace which sternly
keeps the ghosts at bay.

I will not be afraid
as he reminds me
of passions and
deepest reveries.
"Sono una poeta"
he who's with the
truest of melodies.

CAS MCDOWELL

parco delle terme

centuries old and weather-worn,
    the wooden platform
upon which I sit offers
    weary travelers
the space for rest and contemplation.

I am but the most recent of
    these travelers,
resting for a moment, observing
    the swaths
of travelers & poets & artists who,
    like myself, traveled here
in noble pursuit of an ancient
    act of creation,
to absorb the immense blessings
    this world offers,
to respond, to affirm, to seek out
    hidden meaning.

as venus emerged from her
    swooning seafoam,
we too emerge, extending
    the sacrifice,
the knife bloodied, our hands
    still shuddering
with the memory of it.

I will hollow out this heavy
    heart of mine,
scrape out the chambers—
    trawl along
the bottoms of every ocean,
    excavate
each hidden grove, extract
    every last drop
of ambrosia nectar.

EMMA CONLON

117

VI. Deja Vu

A moment from a dream,
One combined where I find
You waltzing down the
Corridor over to me.
How you're not here,
When I know you have
Been before. It must mean
That our souls are familiar here.
So as a ghost you'll travel
With me down these
White travertine halls.

A litttle wine drunk on a bus in Tuscany,
05.07.22

I look around me at all
the different people on this trip
We're walking together right now,
but on vastly different journeys at the same time
There's some kind of magic around us,
and it's not just the place

Everyone brings their own unique brand of magic,
there's colour everywhere

It's blinding, it's intense, it's warm
I don't know where each of us will go,
I don't even know if we'll ever see each other again, but

Right here, right now, it doesn't really matter

This time we've been given together is a gift
And it will live in us forever

Sono un poeta

THIS IS WHAT WE'RE LIVING BY
WHILE WE WALK THROUGH HISTORY.

Sono un poeta.

LOCALS GREET US
WITH SUN-SCARRED SMILES
AND A SMALL WAVE
AND ASK US WHO WE ARE.

ONE BY ONE, WE ANSWER,

Sono un poeta,

AND FOR THE FIRST TIME
SINCE I STARTED TO WRITE POETRY,
WHEN I SAY THIS,
I BELIEVE IT.

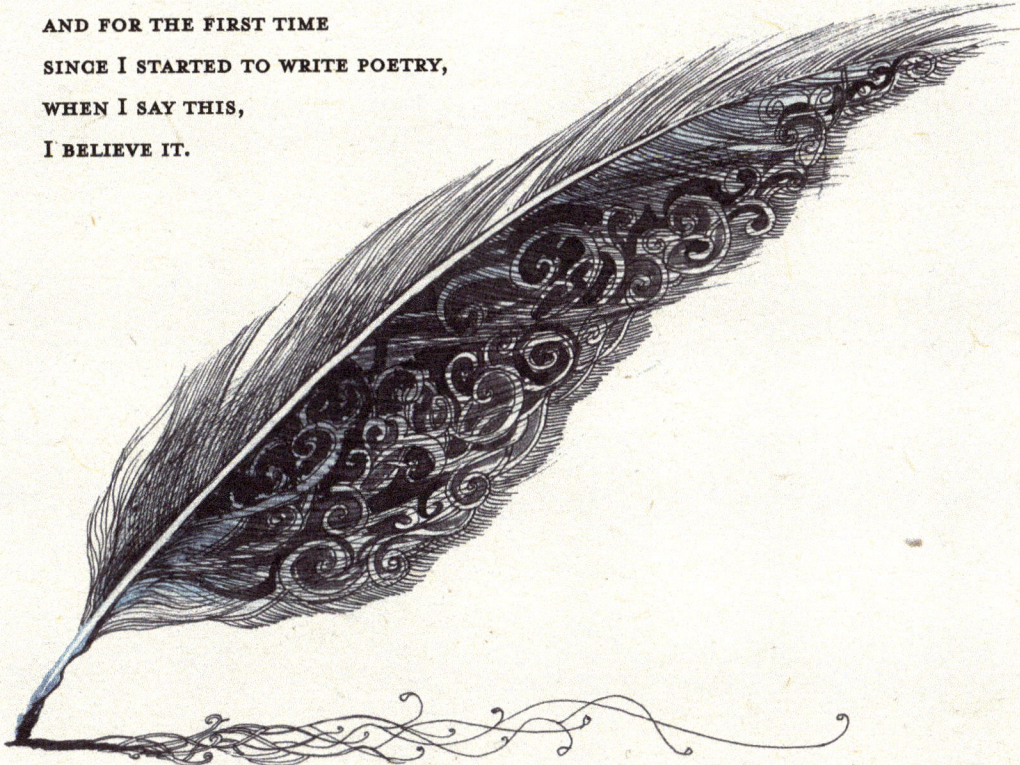

FREYDIS LOVA

I 113 *Castello del Trebbio*

This restored 12th Century castle surrounded by olive trees, vineyards, and gorgeous Tuscan hills is now a center for wine-making and agriculture.

In the past, it was once the site of a turbulent time in Florence's history. The infamous Pazzi family hatched their conspiracy to overthrow the powerful Medici within the castle, but they ultimately failed, and the family was banished— their property and lands confiscated.

After many generations, the castle was restored and brought to life as a place of community, family, and traditional wine and food.

BAD WINE

Today I cooked
In a castle
With a man named jerry.

Today I made food,
For myself,
For my friends.

If they only knew.....
That I haven't cooked in years.
If they only knew,
The trauma residue
Left on my fingernails
As I crack the eggs
Mixing the eggs and flour.
The calming peace washing over me,
I was surprised.

See I know how to cook.
I can do it with my eyes closed.
Which is what I did for 6 years
6 nights a week.

Only allowed to eat out once a week,
And still, he says,
Bae, you can cook this better.

I add more flour to my dough
My hands tingling
As I start to knead.

Sometimes I'd come home late
And he'd be sitting there waiting
I'm hungry he'd whine,
I need to eat.

I knead folding it now,

Why did you buy a cooked chicken?
You know how to cook a chicken,
You just wasted 2 dollars.

I stood frozen in the kitchen
Feeling the ball and chain
Tightly wrapped around my ankle
Leading to the oven.

I stop kneading as Jerry
Shows an incredible way
To cut up the pasta.

Broken I still cook
Even after another starts to feed him.

I pull the knife up as jerry showed me,
The pasta cascades down.
I slide the knife to the right
And the pasta cascades down to the board,

Am I leaving?
What are we doing?
Are we fighting for this?

Well, you're my best friend, he says,
I've loved you more
Than I have ever loved anything,
And you clean
And cook for me......

I feel the chain around my ankle break.
I stand and walk away from the kitchen,
I haven't been back since.

I make a nest
With my perfectly cut noodles.

MELISSA DAVID

126

For years I starve
Afraid of the ball and chain,
Angry at the pots and pans,
Discussed by the spices,
Outraged by the knives.

Yet here I am
Cooking
In a castle
For my friends
For myself

And for the first time,
In a long time,
It feels good.

Thank you, Jerry.

Couscous, semolina

Conchiglie

Farfalle

Ravioli,
tortellini

Rotelle

Semolina, stelline

Spaghetti

MELISSA DAVID

Tagliatelle,
fettuccine

Ravioli,
tortellini

HOME MADE PASTA
Ingredients for 2 persons:
Eggs 2
Flour 1 cup
EV Olive Oil 2 coffe spoon
Salt

Preparation:
Put the flour on a wooden board in the shape of a volcano, and place the eggs in the middle. Add the extra virgin olive oil and some salt. Start mixing the eggs, using a fork, taking the flour from the sides, little by little, so it does not become lumpy. Then start mixing the dough using your hands (remove any rings!). Do not work it too much, as the pasta must stay porous, so as to absorb the sauce better. When the dough has a homogeneous texture, leave it to rest for at least half an hour. Start rolling out the dough: first by hand, then using the rolling-pin. Put a handful of flour on the dough in order to roll it out better, otherwise it risks sticking to your hand and to the rolling pin.
Turn the dough once in a while in order to give it a round and not an oval shape. When the dough becomes very thin (1-2 mm), let it rest again for another half an hour. Then fold the dough and cut it to prepare your preferred pasta shape: tagliatelle are wide stripes, tagliolini are skinny stripes. Open up the stripes, and let them dry.

Recommended pairing:
Toscana IGT Pazzino Castello del Trebbio
Toscana IGT De' Pazzi Castello del Trebbio
Chianti Rùfina Riserva DOCG Lastricato Castello del Trebbio

MEAT SAUCE
Ingredients for 2 person:
Sausage 2
Peeled tomatoes 200 gr
EV Olive Oil
Onion, Bay leaves, Garlic, Rosemary,
Salt, Pepper

Preparation:
Sauté some onion, bay leaves and rosemary in a pan with extra virgin olive oil. Then add the fresh sausage: when the meat becomes golden brown colour, add peeled tomatoes. Let it boil on a low flame for about an hour and a half.

Recommended pairing:
Chili Pepper oil to add a touch of spiciness.

VEGETARIAN SAUCE
Ingredients:
EV Olive Oil
Shallot, Celery,
Thyme and Basil
Carrots
Zucchini
fresh cream
Salt, Pepper

Preparation:
Put some shallot (a type of onion) in a pan with extra virgin olive oil and after a few minutes add grated celery. Add grated carrots and zucchini, some thyme and some fresh basil. Add some fresh cream, and chili (if desired).

Recommended pairing:
Chili Pepper Oil to add a touch of spiciness.
Lemon scented Oil to add freshness.

The century bell

If I die without dreams unfinished,
then I died earlier than my time of death.

This little red car outside of
Castello del Trebbio says "Where
dreams never end." which felt very
fitting for this magical trip.

— R.

CATHERINE PITTS

I see in front of me a survivor

safe, sober, and surrounded by those who love her

as she was always meant to be

She sings like an angel despite the demons she has defeated

I can not help but to be speechless

for what words are there for someone

who has come so far and seen so much most will never know

J.S.

5th july, 2022

i cried today. the type where you have found the acknowledgment of coming home to yourself. it has only been the second day of being here, and i feel like i'm just becoming more and more speechless with every passing moment. i want to stay as still as i could possibly can, and flow with the nature of things. no words, or movement. do you ever have the feeling where something so incredible is unfolding before your eyes, and it feels like you can't absorb it enough? don't even blink; you'll miss something that will shift your world. that's how i've been feeling, honestly. we had our very first workshop today at the stunning Parco delle Terme. it was a structure of an ancient roman bath, and there's a little park area in the middle. the tiled murals and water springs are gorgeous. rachel started us off with her beautiful words, and then essentially "let us into the wild" within the space of the park. we sat, thought, explored, wrote, painted, observed and marvelled.

i didn't think i would write anything, but i decided to reach into myself and hold the hand of a pain i've hidden in the shadows. it gripped me hard. i took a breath and wrote, and then the tears fell. i exhaled, and the grip lessen. rachel came around to check on me after that, and i showed her my poem. she held my hand and cried with me. "never stop writing". i think i've waited five years to hear that. i didn't think she'd say that. i didn't think that i could do all i've ever wanted, but they were always just right there.

映月

KAITLYN YÍNG YUÉ

July 6th

Florence

These days continue to surprise me. My workshop this morning was about Ekphrasis poetry, one of my favorite forms of writng. It's basically a conversation between poetry and art. It's origins date back to ancient Greece— and since we were to visit Michelangelo's David today— I knew it would be perfect.

After my lesson on Ekphrasis poetry, I opened up the floor to create a sharing space of sorts where my poets could read pieces they've written on this trip, or long before. Many of them came up and sat beside me to read their poetry aloud, some of them— for the first time. I held Kaitlyn's hand as she read her poem— I'm so incredibly proud of her. I wonder if she knows how brave she is.

After sharing poems, we took a day trip into Florence, and what a whirlwind it was! Lucia was our city guide and she was phenomenal. At one point she looked at us and said "David is waiting for you" and it seemed like the most promising sentence in the world. More than anything, I desperately wanted my poets to see the unfinished scultpures that accompany David. As you approach him, Michelangelo's Prisoners line the wall.

There is so much poetry to be found in them, and when I saw my poets stopping and staring at the prisoners more than David, my heart leapt. I feel so understood by them. They get me! They think like me! They see poetry in the world and they capture it! What a dream, what a spectacular dream.

R. CLIFT

July 6

AFTER OUR REGULAR BREAKFAST CLUB, WE MET IN THE GLASS ATRIUM OF THE hotel between the lobby and the pool for our next workshop. It was bright and all the furniture was red and gold. Big leafy potted palms and ferns cast shadowy stripes over us and brushed our shoulders as we settled into a corner.

Rachel first taught about Ekphrasis Poetry— it would be fun to play with later when we visited museums, she explained.

Then it was time to share poems, old or new, if one wanted to. There wasn't pressure to read, of course. Rachel and I decided long ago that we would meet artists where they were and support everyone how they needed as an individuals. We started clockwise and one by one each traveler sat up front beside Rachel and shared work they loved, that meant a lot, that was in progress. A few didn't feel up to sharing yet and that was ok— we all gained a sacred kind of kinship from witnessing each artist speak their words, sometimes for the first time.

The atrium was humming with poetry when we left it. Our journey of the day was to visit the beautiful and artistic city of Florence. Once we arrived we met a few of Federica's friends within the jewelry and leather shops of Piazza di Santa Croce. They were all very kind and sold lovely handcrafted items. We then met our city guide, Lucia, in the square and walked with her from Santa Croce to Uffizi. It is here where I feel the heart of Florence resides.

Local artists set up stands in the courtyard of the celebrated museum and I was glad to see a few familiar artists that I recognized from my previous visit in 2017 and 2019. Everything had changed— yet the art had not. It was comforting.

We continued past the fantastic Ponte Vecchio— a bridge straight from a fantasy story with little pink, blue, and yellow fairy houses clinging to the sides. We passed buildings of Renaissance architecture that seemed unassuming, but then Lucia would tell us that Leonardo da Vinci spent his childhood within the walls we stood before now. History was palpable.

The Duomo was brilliant in the sun, the white, green and pink marbled almost iridescent. Our final stop was the Galleria Accademia- Lucia led us through the gallery of paintings providing insight into each and around the corridor to see Michealangelo's *David* standing proud in the soft midday light. Before the celebrated figure stood five other sculptures— all unfinished. Forms that were almost chipped away to be human stretched desperately to be freed from the marble but they were frozen in time long ago. These works were called *Michelangelo's Prisoners*.

XII

The contrast between the rough stone and the finished masterpiece high-lighted how incredible the *David* truly is. There is almost a warmth under the cool marble skin- a suggestion of life caught beneath gossamer layers of stone. As if one could reach out, touch his hand, and feel a pulse.

We were set free in the gallery to wander and I stood to draw the *David*. Each time I visit the gallery I draw the statue from life. I have since 2017— so I suppose I'll go on doing it. It's a personal marker of the passage of time for me, now.

We all meandered back towards Santa Croce in separate little groups. Some went to stationary shops for dip pens and ink, others to find gelato. We met back in the square for dinner at a restaurant on the Piazza called Boccadama.

It wasn't originally part of our itinerary— but Federica had thought it would be lovely to spend more time in Florence and once we all agreed she arranged the whole dinner that day. She truly added such skill and joy to the experience.

We enjoyed some of the best food of the whole trip. Fresh bruschetta and a local favorite of prosciutto e melone. We chose from truffle ravioli, carbonara, and the best pesto I've ever had. Federica introduced us to chocolate salami— a kind of sweet composed of a chocolate ganache and biscotti pieces.

The way home involved a walk along the Arno river as the sun dipped behind the green hills. Ancient buildings on either side of the verdant foliage shined like the jewels on velvet we'd seen earlier that day.

Firenze cannot be captured in a single day— but it only takes that short amount of time to fall in love with it and vow to return.

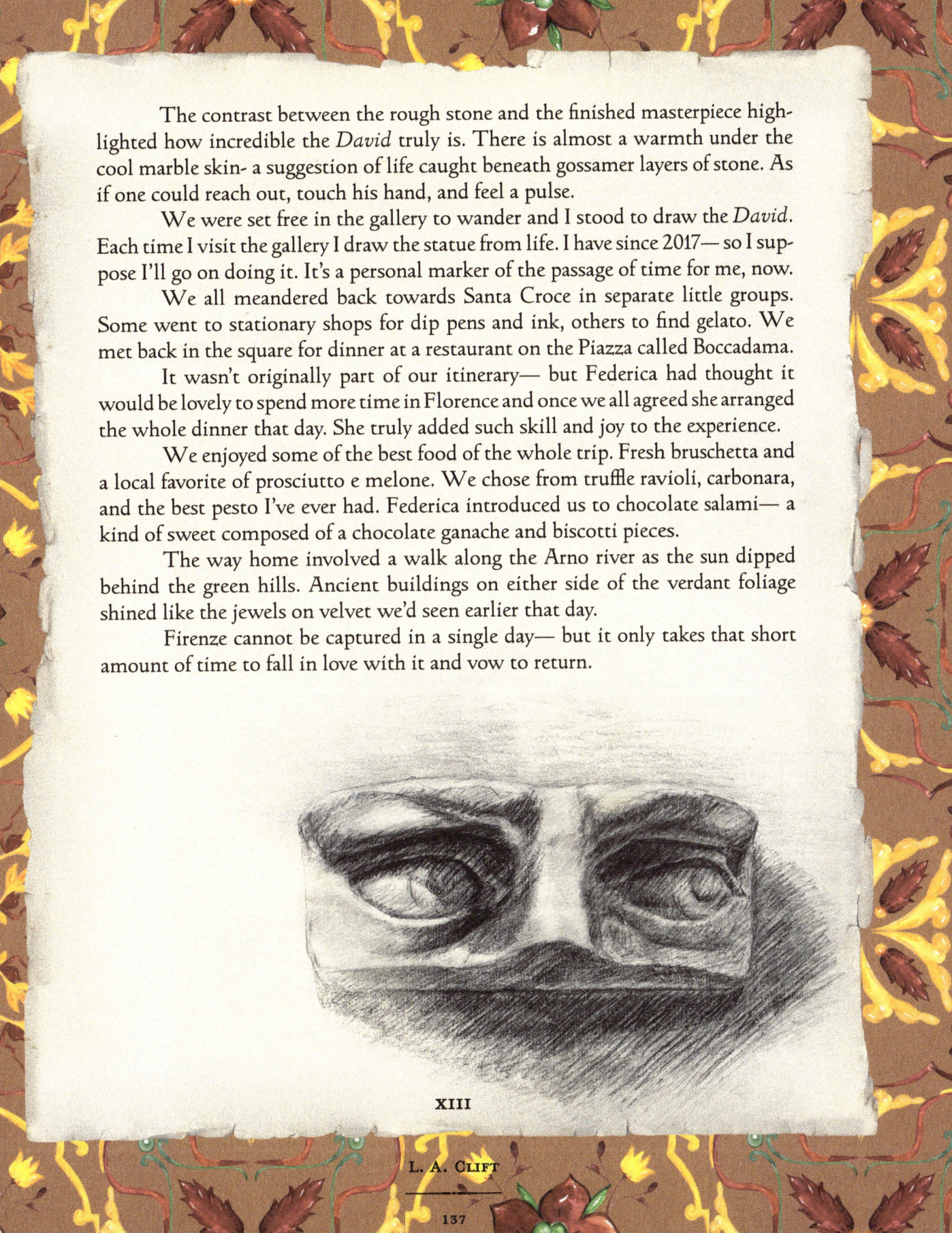

XIII

il suon che di dolcezza i sensi lega

I heard your symphony this morning
in the coo of the doves, the metrical hum
of the cicadas, shimmering like an oasis
in the arid summer heat. the light pitching
through a skylight stained with the centuries
of dust and storms, fading in the tuscan sun.
our angels fly above the paneled glass of ambers,
willow greens and dusty oranges in coronation.
each fluid arm flawlessly posed in perfectly
preserved dance, a flurry of ivory wings,
graceful limbs, unveiling your secret melody.
birds join them in their dance, flitting up
from their pear trees, their elegant fountains
happily bubbling in the sun. the muses too
call down to me as they called out to you,
leaning out their terraced balconies
on sophisticated limbs. the women cup
their ears to hear the music just as I do,
their fluttering hair of auburn flames
and golden fields of rye ripple in the same
breeze tucking my hair behind my ear.
we are here, together, in this moment.
in some sense, we will always be here
in this moment together, swaying with
the trees, enjoying our painter's symphony—
the enchanting angels, the muses in their
refined gowns of periwinkles and corals,
pink fingertips reaching out to touch
our shared painted horizons. and I, grounded,
tethered to this earth, an entrapment
beyond their comprehension. we parallel,
coalesce, imitate. I leave them behind,
secure in their palace of carved marble.
we are both bound to our eternities.
how long they will last, we cannot say.
I am a mere blip in their existence, we two
lines crossing at this cosmic junction.

I am grateful for your hospitality.

EMMA CONLON

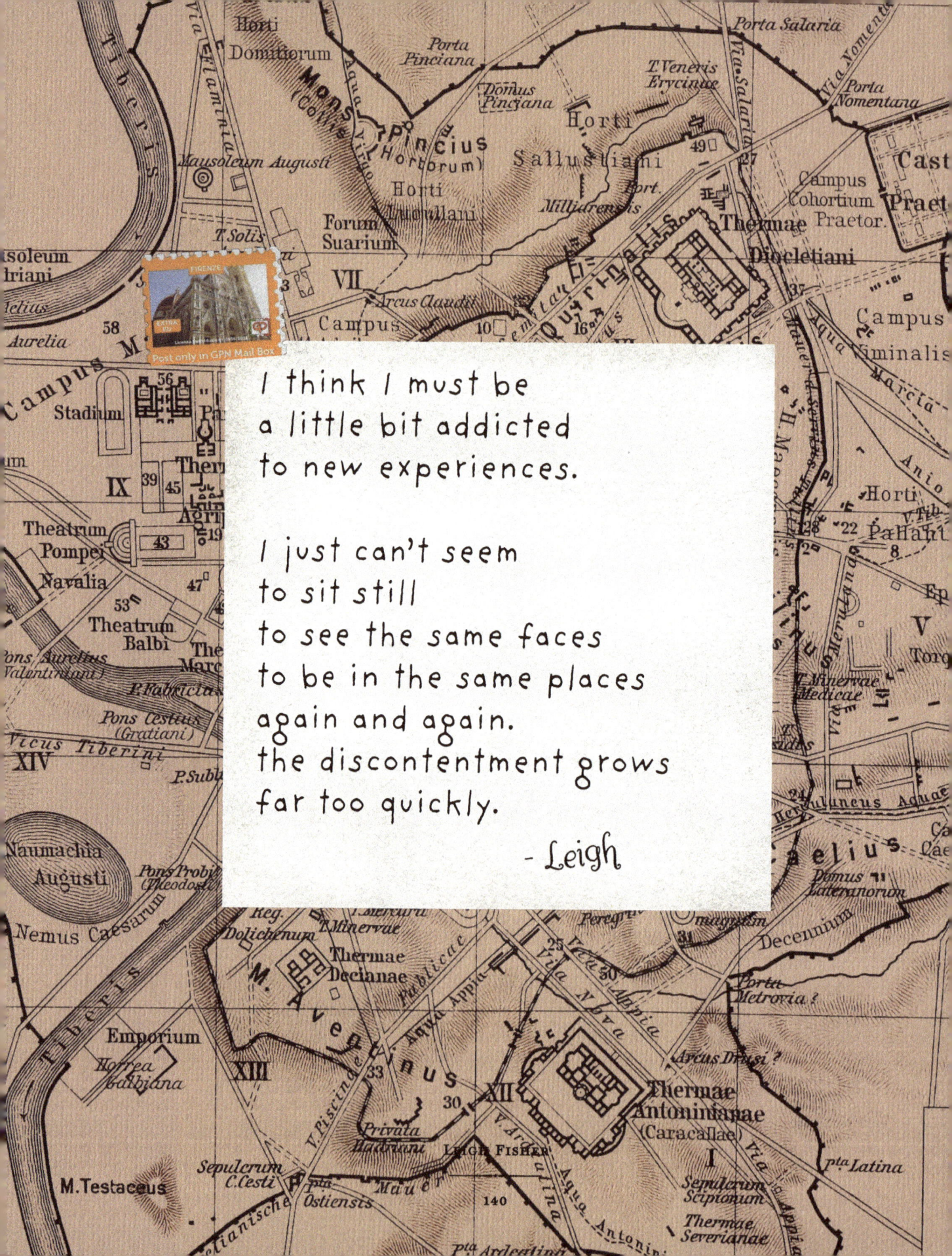

I think I must be
a little bit addicted
to new experiences.

I just can't seem
to sit still
to see the same faces
to be in the same places
again and again.
the discontentment grows
far too quickly.

- Leigh

VIII.

how do you always do this to me?
rip my heart out to show
who I really can be.

you're Home. you're Magic.
you're Everything and more.
you're Love. you're Hope.
you're Hurt and Anger, too.

red roofs, tall cyprus trees,
and leading lines of vines,
are this Place. this Dream.
I fight to reclaim and call
all Mine.

I never want to leave -
I never want to lose
- this Wildflower I am.
the one who feels the
Sun and Blooms.

Let me stay, and let me live.
Oh, dear Tuscany,

Please let me breathe.

CAS MCDOWELL

half of me

There are a million half-written poems
in half-filled notebooks
stacked on shelves
that I put a half-assed effort into building

And within all these poems
lies only half my heart

Because I wrote them
from half-felt emotions
stemming from
my half-lived human life

Honestly
I think for when you read my words
you'd only learn half
of who I truly am

It's just like when my friends
pick up the phone to call me
and I only tell them half the truth
so I burden them
with only half my hurt

And sometimes I wonder
if half of anything
will ever be enough

I mean, it must be
because I have heard the stories
of people who have traveled
halfway around the world
to meet the loves of their lives
against all odds

And those who see the glass half-full
referred to as the optimistic ones

And even under the light
of a half-lit moon
there's still enough energy
to pull the tides

JENNIFER GELLOCK

142

that sustains the rhythm
of all our human lives

But if I'm being truly honest
I think I've always known
that half of anything
will never be enough

Because when I hold
myself back
I know I'm only
halfway to freedom

I've learned
that half-filled promises
will only break others hearts

And that half-lived dreams
won't move me closer
to fulfilling my ultimate destiny

Honestly
I think for when my last day
comes to live
I think I'd be sad
if I completed only half
my Earthly tasks

Now

there are a million half-written poems
in half-filled notebooks
stacked on shelves
that I put a half-assed effort into building

And at the heart
of all of these half done things
I've finally learned
it was just the fear of being fully seen

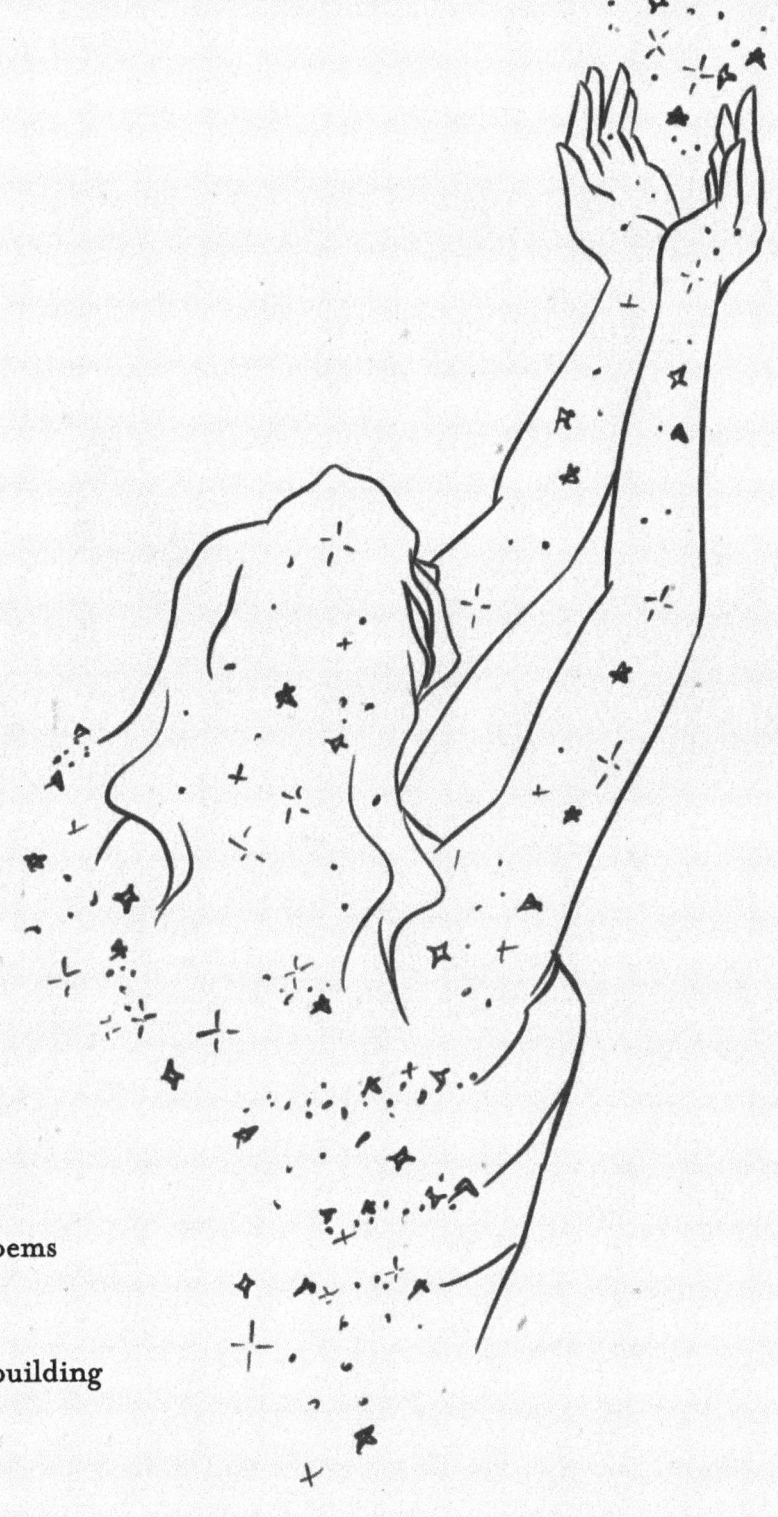

JENNIFER GELLOCK

[Note: Performed on July 7th at an impromptu sharing space in the hotel lobby. Illustration by Laura Clift.]

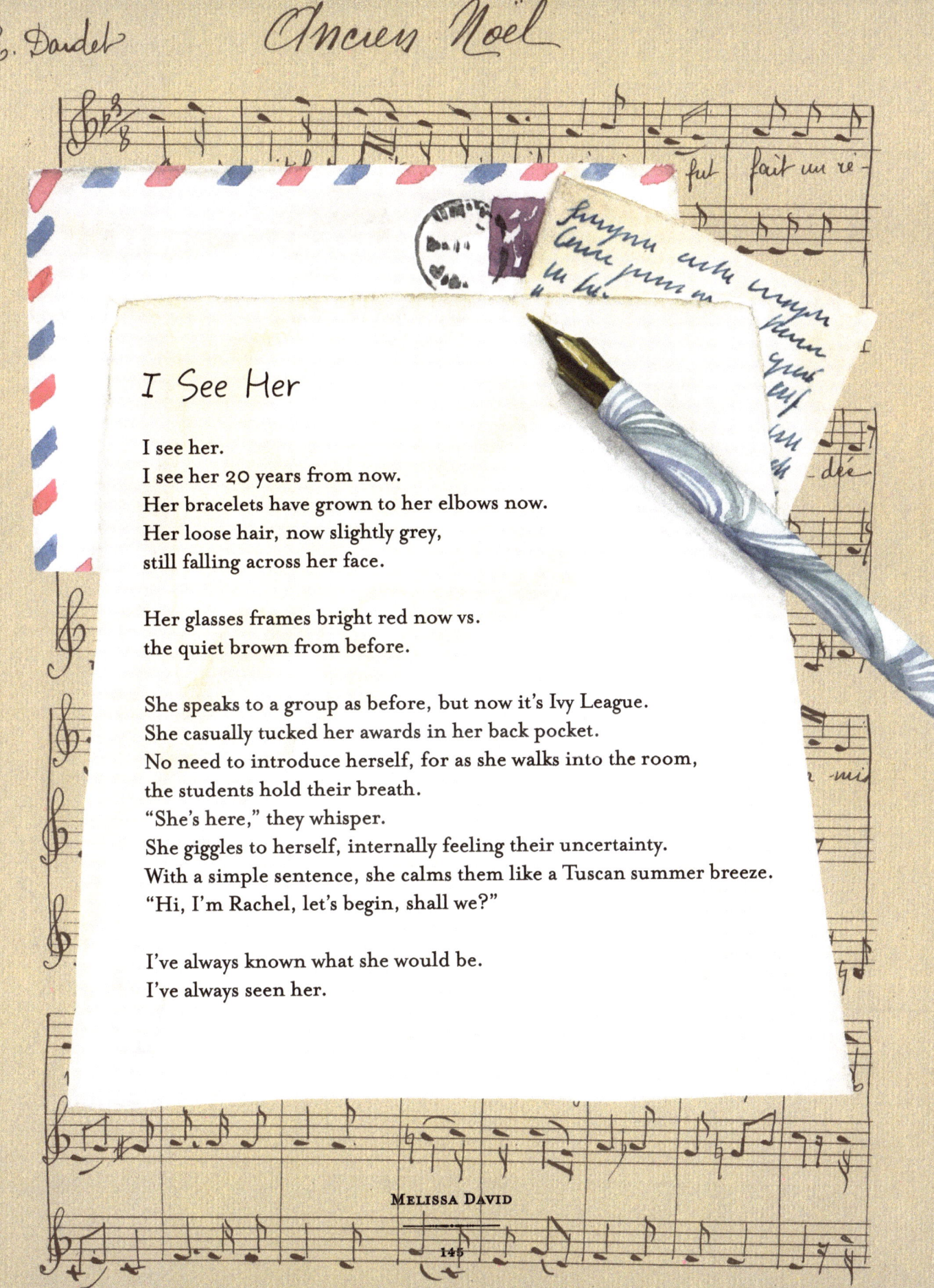

I See Her

I see her.
I see her 20 years from now.
Her bracelets have grown to her elbows now.
Her loose hair, now slightly grey,
still falling across her face.

Her glasses frames bright red now vs.
the quiet brown from before.

She speaks to a group as before, but now it's Ivy League.
She casually tucked her awards in her back pocket.
No need to introduce herself, for as she walks into the room,
the students hold their breath.
"She's here," they whisper.
She giggles to herself, internally feeling their uncertainty.
With a simple sentence, she calms them like a Tuscan summer breeze.
"Hi, I'm Rachel, let's begin, shall we?"

I've always known what she would be.
I've always seen her.

MELISSA DAVID

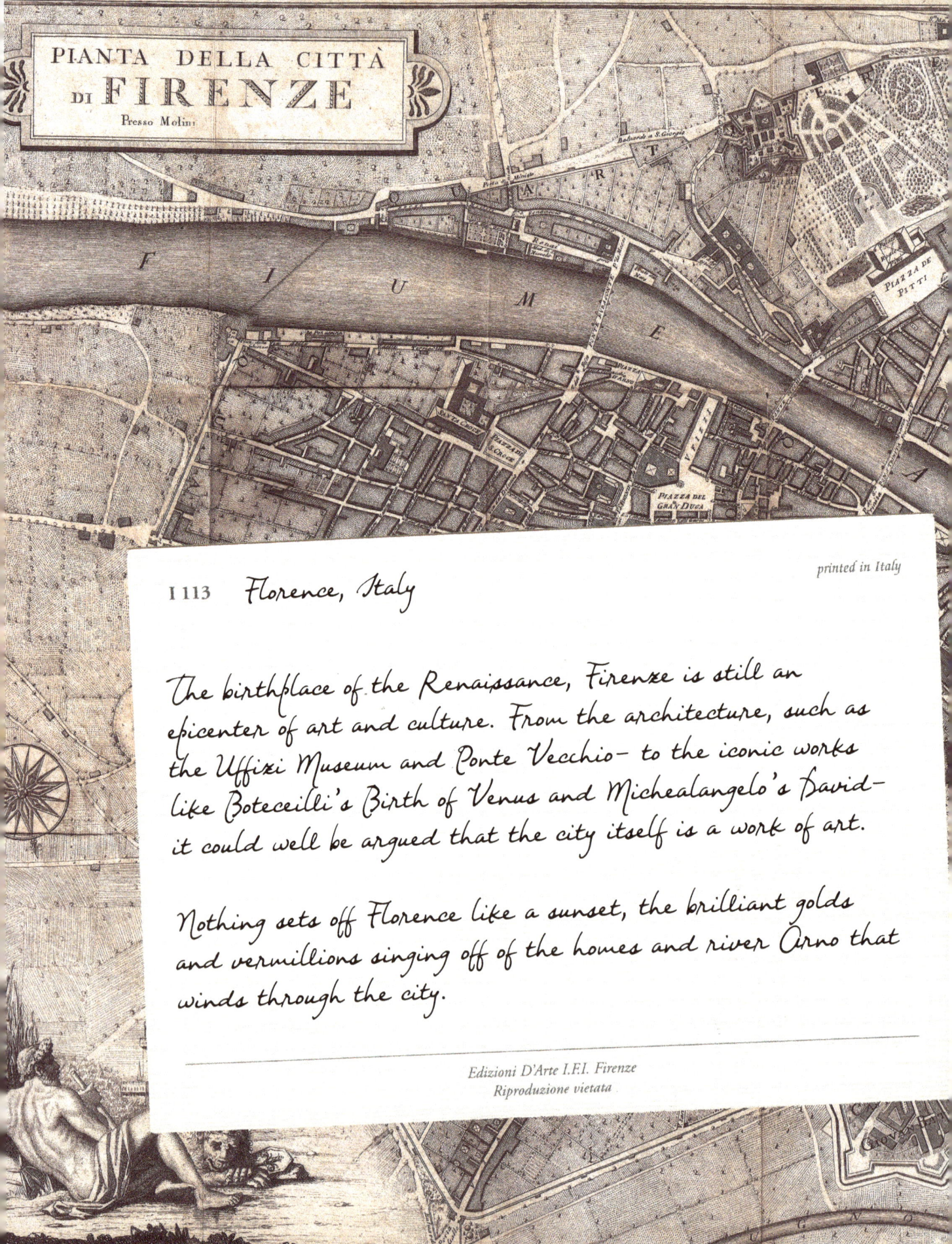

Florence, Italy

printed in Italy

The birthplace of the Renaissance, Firenze is still an epicenter of art and culture. From the architecture, such as the Uffizi Museum and Ponte Vecchio— to the iconic works like Boteceilli's Birth of Venus and Michealangelo's David— it could well be argued that the city itself is a work of art.

Nothing sets off Florence like a sunset, the brilliant golds and vermillions singing off of the homes and river Arno that winds through the city.

Edizioni D'Arte I.F.I. Firenze
Riproduzione vietata

Art & Poetry Workshop Two

Lucia

Quotes from Lucia, our guide
around the city of Florence

"You are young. You are brave."

"Michelangelo is waiting for you."

"David and Pietà we're not born under a lucky star."

"The way Michelangelo viewed sculpture is that
a living creature was trapped in the core of the marble
and it was his task to free them
by removing the heavy material—

It represents his view on the human condition,
how the soul longs to be free from the bonds of flesh."

Lucia

I heard your name out loud for the first time in over ten years

"Lucia"

It pierced my heart as I was transported back to a cool wooden floor
of an echoing basketball gymnasium
And there you were with your earbuds getting pumped-up to Billy Joel classics
Everytime I think back on your pre-game rituals - I laugh
Still today, when *Piano Man* echoes through my radio dial
I look up to the Heaven's and smile

Coach always tried to get our attention
because together we often chose to sing and dance
through the drills at practice rather than dribble
I remember the day we hosted a spaghetti fundraiser dinner
at your grandparents' authentic Italian restaurant
And your mom's bold Italian voice cheering us on
from the stands yelling madly at the refs, she was our biggest fan

After our final season we rarely kept in touch
And we were okay with that
It was one of those friendships that was sacred and held between
the baselines of the hardwood where all our memories were stored

Today, I'm here in Italy and I've heard your name over and over again
ringing through the city streets of Florence

"Lucia, Lucia"

It brought back to the day in my early twenties when I heard the news
about your gentle soul, a favorite soul of mine,
who chose to take their human life too soon

They told me you left to liberate yourself
so you could love just who you wanted
Free from la famiglia and the Catholic Church's judgment

JENNIFER GELLOCK

150

So, as I walked these streets of Florence
I did so in your honor and prayed that you are up there flying high
cradled in the arms of your Italian ancestors

I looked for you here
I even shed a tear for you here
As I looked up to the Heavens
I asked my friend Mel to sing for you a Billy Joel classic here

And as the wind picked-up my sundress and the rain poured down
over the streets of Florence, I held out my hand
and I felt your innocent presence in every drop of sadness from the clouds

Then within minutes the sun came back out and I began to dance
to Billy Joel's *Piano Man*

Saluté to you, my dearest friend Lucia,
may you shower the light within my heart over the city of Florence forever

JENNIFER GELLOCK

[Note: Written about a dear friend of mine from grade school growing up]

the leather market

federica brings us to a leather shop
    attached to a gold market
in piazza santa croce. we enjoy
    the demonstration, enjoy
the leather bags with hidden pockets,
    reversible belts with gold & silver
buckles, gold leaf embossed journals,
    maroon & emerald & royal blue,
the grace kelly bag with its golden
    clasp in any color you might want.
the room is aromatic with the earthy
    oiled leather, oaken and almost,
almost sweet. the oils and waxes
    taking a dull sheen in the light.

I buy a brown leather backpack
    with brass zippers. the salesperson
takes me to the back of the store,
    assures me the man we are about
to meet is a rare breed these days,
    "not too many people remaining
who can do what he can by hand."
    said handiwork is impressive. he
stamps my initials in gold on
    the backpack, sealing the thin
metal sheet in with tools worn
    & cracked with age, heated to
the same temperature he's trained
    his ears to know the sizzle of.
he takes my red leather bookmark

EMMA CONLON

(an impulse-buy at checkout)
& stamps it too with my initials,
   this time silver to match the small
intricate designs he embossed himself.
   silver, he says. to match the prior
adornments. & there is something
   so ordinary & so magic about it.
this italian man in an italian leather
   shop in piazza santa croce. the
ordinariness of this practiced routine,
   year after year after year. the magic
of a master craftsman performing
   & the slow final bow of his artform.

EMERY CONLON

153

Stones

The raindrops hit the ancient stones
She rests her palms against their warmth
To catch the raindrops
She is thirsty

Lost in time

A Quiet Love

There is such a
love between us.

A quiet love.

MELISSA DAVID

154

A person picks not their passion
anymore do they choose
what the weather of the world will be.

J.S.

J.S.

the grasshopper

the sky rips herself into pieces,
and all that ache pours down
to flood piazzale degli uffizi.

it's raining outside the uffizi
and we take cover behind
the stone columns, browse

paintings displayed by the
usual street artists.

it's raining outside the uffizi
and I feel like we are in a
painting again. the rippling

puddles, raindrops splashing
in neptune's fountain.

you offer to share your
umbrella, the precious little
coverage it offers divided

between the two of us.
maybe you noticed how I
clutched my bag to my chest

to protect the art I kept
safe inside of it.

maybe it is natural to you,
this small kindness, but it
means so, so much to me.

EMMA CONLON

156

it is in this very moment
my brain begins

composing this poem to you.
I am trying to unearth those
words I could not find then.

later, we find a grasshopper
basking in the new sun on
a pole supporting velvet rope

outside of the galleria
dell'accademia.

and for you, my pointing
that grasshopper out to
you was thanks enough.

EMMA CONLON

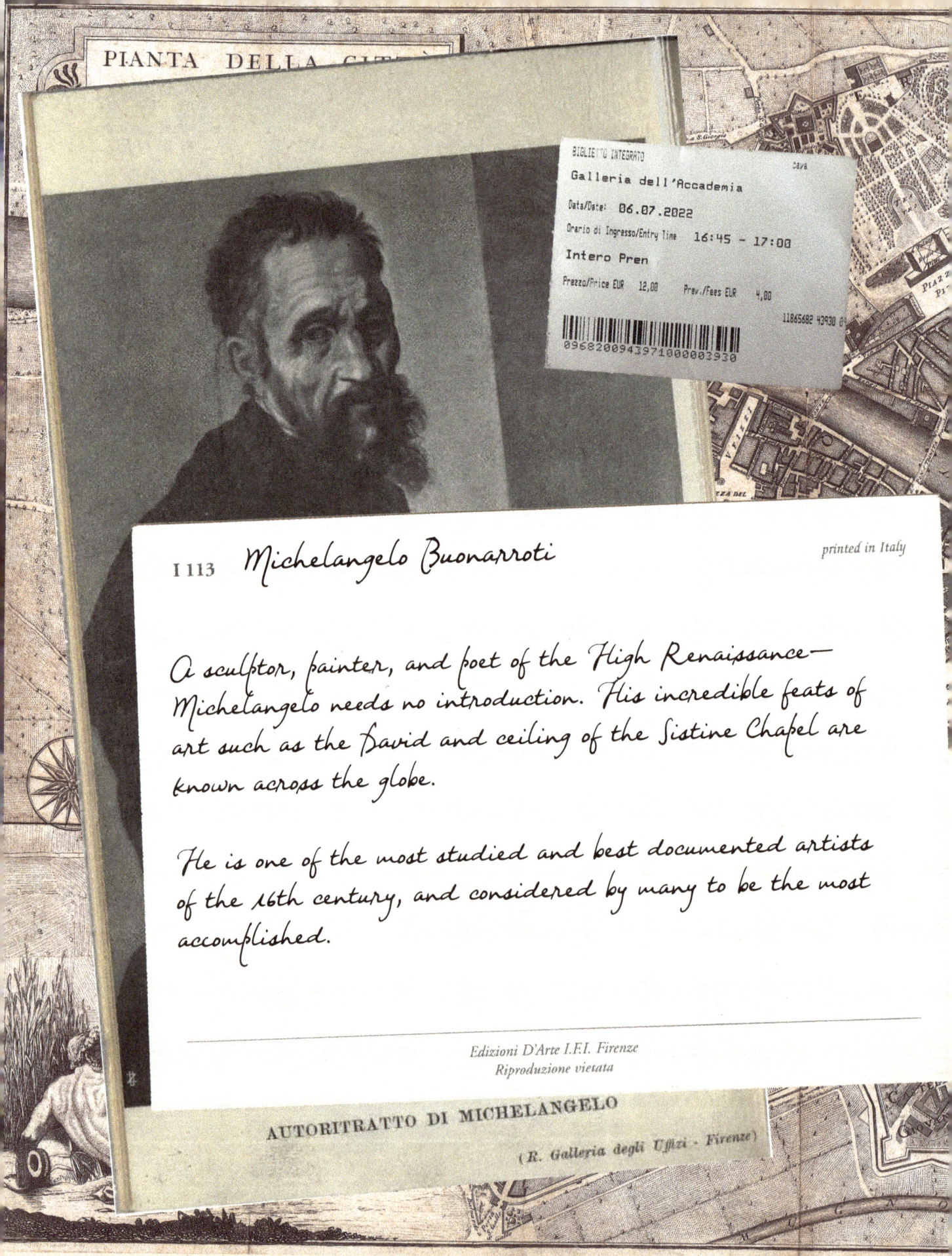

Galleria dell'Accademia

Data/Date: 06.07.2022

Orario di Ingresso/Entry Time   16:45 - 17:00

Intero Pren

Prezzo/Price EUR   12,00   Prev./Fees EUR   4,00

11865682 43930 0

0968200943971000003930

I 113   *Michelangelo Buonarroti*

A sculptor, painter, and poet of the High Renaissance—Michelangelo needs no introduction. His incredible feats of art such as the David and ceiling of the Sistine Chapel are known across the globe.

He is one of the most studied and best documented artists of the 16th century, and considered by many to be the most accomplished.

AUTORITRATTO DI MICHELANGELO

(R. Galleria degli Uffizi - Firenze)

Laura's sketch of David

Capturing This Moment

"I wish I could capture this moment with my words."

The big blue sky is crowded by massive cathedral walls,
thousand year old statues stare into my soul,
visitors form different lands chatter in their native tongues,
the smell of a recent rainfall fills the air,
 a distant cello,
 "grazzi" at every turn,
this town makes my cheeks curl towards the sun

As I walked I saw Florence's century bell that rings at each turn.
I thought for me to make it to year 3000 is a stretch,
but to die without dreams is to have died before living your last breath.

 I linger at all the art,
to catch a glimpse of the old carved expressions.
I stretch to my toes as my tired body keeps up with my curious mind.
And I am told it's time to stand in line,
to meet David.

A long time ago a famous artist made him.
I learned he was created to be the ideal man.
 "These are some shoes to fill," I thought.

It was time,
I entered the museum
turned a corner
and there...
beyond the schools of fish,
and decorative art,
stands him,
David.
A statue so tall with the most grandiose skylight,
David.

I walked closer and glared at his chiseled jaw in awe,
Then reality kicked in,
 and I walked promptly to a bench behind David
to rest my tired, very human, legs.

CATHERINE PITTS

160

I couldn't help but wonder if part of my awe came from all the talk,
the prestigious descriptions and the crowds disposition.
Not much has changed,
with the "ideal man" still being fake.

Before I left, I found a man named The Atlas.
He didn't have a face,
instead he carried a very large weight.

They say his work was never finished,
that he's a slave stuck in stone.

I related to this man,
 I knew how he felt.
But he is frozen in time,
and I still had mine.

I left for dinner,
taking in delicious views.

 This dinner was one of a kind,
I learned the Italians have a thing,
a certain forte, so-to-say
Carbs, Spritz, and a hell of a good time.

 The sunset this night was nothing but a dream,
I felt like I was rowing down stream.
This life is was simple,
"Just be and enjoy,
don't carry the weight of the world."

Oh if I could live in this way,
all of my days,
without feeling like a chick stuck in her egg.
but maybe,
if I can just capture this moment,
I will be able to revisit it one day

CATHERINE PITTS

161

I walked down the line
and felt emptiness and cold.
There are voices screaming
in the silence, sobbing and begging
to be let out. So many unfinished lives
gasping for breath in marble, unable to
open mouths that were never formed.
I want to cry with them.
They have no eyes yet I can see their pain.
I want to take their hands in mine
but they have no hands to hold.
There is a distance between us,
greater than the ropes that keep them safe
inside their broken coffins.
Their shackles weigh heavy on my wrists.

I'm sorry.

I can't write for you while I'm here.

You're holding me prisoner,
just as he made you.

FREYDIS LOVA

XV.

Ecco. Andiamo! Rings from the Italian guide's lips. He leads the way, a small hunch in his shoulders, his blue jacket draped. Ecco. He repeats in his mic, your own Jiminy Cricket whispering in your ears. He shows you the stars, the stories before. Ecco, andiamo. You wake from the dream, in Florence you see he was just a ghost you'd once followed before.

CAS McDOWELL

Florence

MELISSA DAVID

MELISSA DAVID

165

the stationary shop

has so much to look at my eyes
don't know where to land:

wooden figurines of venus
& pinocchio; tiny models

of bookshelves & 19th
century puppet shows; the

rows of antique bottles,
rootbeer brown & seafoam

green; slow-spinning mobiles
of the planets & hot air balloons;

cheap prints of famous italian
art, florence's sprawling scenery;

vintage postcards & puzzles;
sealing wax in every color

you can think of in under
a minute, perhaps hundreds

of emblems to stamp it with
(you can pick any color handle

you'd like for the seal, the sign
informs us, nervously flitting

then to *please don't touch, we
will be happy to assist you.);*

heirlooms, magnifying glasses
& compasses in gold-clasped

wooden boxes spread across
a map. you notice me

EMMA CONLON

———————

166

admiring the feather quill I
can't afford after the backpack.

I tell you as much when you
ask. I wander off, distracted

by the beautiful notebooks
& pens. you buy it then,

while I'm distracted—
the quill with a bottle of

royal blue ink. a gift for me,
a person you met mere days

ago. is there not a kind of
magic in a moment like that?

EMMA CONLON

Art as a polymorphic entity

To try to explain
    to someone who cannot see
I would say it is the call of your heart
What consumes your soul
    Elements of life that mirror
    the strength of your will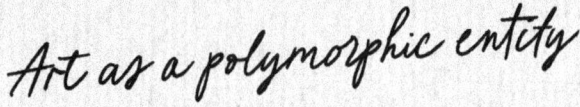

DENAE TERESE

168

She chiseled her name into the center
    of his marble heart
So he could never erase her
The memory of who she was etched
    into him forever
Breaking down the walls
    of his hard exterior
Her softness now lives
    inside him forever

He called out to her -
Ciao Bella!
you are the olive of my heart
that stems from silver sage leaves
with the wisdom
of an aged Italian fine wine

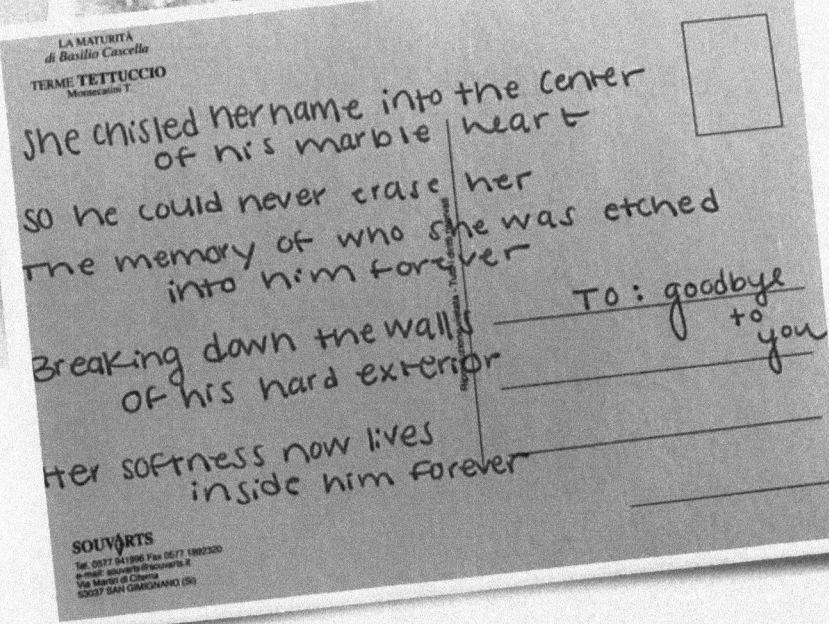

JENNIFER GELLOCK

IX.

Michelangelo, who are you? Your long beard, curled hair, and broken nose. Who are you to have trapped us in this veined, cold stone? Why did you leave? You left us to carry this weight. .The world is heavy. Michelangelo, you were meant to break us free.

But we have to stay. You left but I guess you wished for us to keep your Love's company. Of course he's strapping and tall, but he's just as imprisoned. Michelangelo, you left him with thoughts unable to share your words. Words that only he could ever know.

CAS McDOWELL

X.

David -
You stay under a dome.
A ray in the shape of the star.
Is it you who shines?
Or the dreams that you're holding?

CAS MCDOWELL

pilgrimage

we have a little less than an hour
        to make this strange journey,
freydis and catherine and me,
        weaving through the street
connecting piazza santa croce
        with piazza della signoria,
winding around mercato del
        porcellino, past basilica di
santa trinita and over the bridge
        of the same name. all to
return to gustapizza: captor of
        my adoration. I am on some
mythic, mundane quest to eat
        a gustapizza, my favorite
pizza on the menu. I am the
        ridiculous protagonist of
my own strange adventure. my
        companions entrust their
previous time to me, trust me
        when I tell them that the
best place to get pizza just so
        happens to be across the
street from where I lived three
        years ago. and then, the
memory kicks in—I am walking
        back from art history with
friends to grab a pizza before our
        next class. time travel or
déjà vu or some other matter of
        thing I do not claim to
understand. we order our pizzas,
        watch as servers carry discs
of margherita, cotto e funghi,
        bufalina, carbonara, caprese
and calabrese, and my favorite
        of all: arugala, tomatoes, and
parmesan. the gustapizza. we
        wait, and I show freydis and

catherine my old building. our
       numbers are called. we collect
our prizes. we walk back to meet
       the others in our tour group,
freydis and catherine and me.
       and I think about how lucky
I am to have met people willing
       to give their precious time
to help me find my old favorite
       pizza joint in all of florence,
to accompany me halfway
       across the city to eat pizzas.
I think and we trace back
       across the bridge, past the
statue of justice, the little
       bronze boar, judith, david,
medusa and perseus, heracles.
       we eat our pizzas, ignoring
the justified stares of the people
       we passed by. I'll never forget
that. the kindness of friends
       who are still strangers. a
pilgrimage to gustapizza.

EMMA CONLON

My Girls

I saved the Merchant of Venice Today.
Shoved in a bookshelf,
The broken pieces
In a rare bookstore
50 feet away from the David.

They are closing and trying to get me out
But I found the cover, and I found a picture of Portia,
And I know the manuscript is somewhere.

"We are closing!" They yell again
.... don't they know I actually care!
Don't they know the smell of old books
Warms my ancient soul.

My had slips blindly behind the front layer
Into the depths of dusty time,
My hand presses through eyes closed,

"I found it!" I squeal.

The book is in pieces in my hand
As I walk to the counter
To the confused Italian man
Waiting with his old big black dog.

"10 euros" he says flatly

I place it safely in the bag
next to the intact Italian Hamlet
1874 I found earlier.

I pay the man and he lets us out the side door.
I clutch the bag to my chest and say,
Don't worry Ophelia,
Don't worry Portia,
I'm taking you home.

My feet fall out onto the Florence streets
Just the girls and me.

— Mel

POETI E PROSATORI STRANIERI

G. SHAKESPEARE

IL MERCANTE DI VENEZIA

Traduzione
di
CINO CHIARINI

...omo per l'abitudine di

a bene.

ie.

Antonio si riterrà

...sa più lunga)

esto piacere?
s?

...onio vinco-

SHYLOCK.

buono. (Cioè uomo che b...
persona solvibile)

PORZIA
nella sua cappa nera di «Dottore».

G. SHAKESPEARE

IL MERCANTE DI VENEZIA

TRADUZIONE
DI
CINO CHIARINI

Venezia

bells ringing
gulls crying
musicians singing
outboard engines spluttering
balcony leaves rustling
wind whispering
buildings sighing
canal wakes lapping
away at the walls
of history

This is Venice.

A Venetian Reverie

I'm a little more at peace
among the familiar sound
of gull cries
and the new melody
of bells ringing

can I lose myself
in the history
of an island city
where you can always
find your way home?

LEIGH FISHER

I needed to come back
to a city unreal as a dream

I returned wounded
by all of life's tiny casualties—
small limitations—
and little devastations

I always lose sight
of what I want most
as unrealistic as
my pipe dream may be

but back in this city
unreal as a dream
I remember not all dreams
turn into nightmares

and if an island city can survive
the changing of the tides
then surely
so can I

LEIGH FISHER

I 113 *Basilica of Santa Croce*

printed in Italy

With a gorgeous facade of cream, sage green, and pale terracotta marble— the Basilica of Santa Croce is much like a small mirror of the grand Duomo.

Inside you will find tombs of many famous Florentines, such as Galileo Galilei, Niccolò Machiavelli, and Michaelangelo.

Carbonara

I'm crying over Carbonara
This isn't a poem
Just letting you know
I'm having the best Carbonara
Surrounded by the city of Florence at
Baccadoma est 1996
Now for Melon covered prosciutto
for dessert
If you need directions,
Please see below.

MELISSA DAVID

XVII. Vinciane

Qui est-elle? Who is she?
This glowing, lonesome woman who sits staring back at me. Her eyes hold a glimmer, one that shines like a Tuscan sunrise. She's summer and sweet, with a wrap in her hair, what stories does she desire to share with me?

Qui est-elle? Who is this wonder?
A wanderer who travels alone. From Brussels to France, then right here in Florence.
Santa Croce behind us is no beauty compared to she. Perhaps because one day I long to be the woman at the table staring back at a wild, adventurous younger me. To be called teacher, lover, and friend. To traverse across borders, to hug them and hold their hands.

And even now, dear Vinciane est Elle. She still desires the world, with that green guidebook in her hands. Oh what a wonder. Let me grow up to behold life as Vinciane certainly has.

CAS McDOWELL

181

Steadfast Love

My love for you holds me steadfast
in a world constantly turning.
Teach me your ways,
it's for you I live all my days.
May your spirit lead me
and hold me,
in the midst of so much change.

CATHERINE PITTS

Girasole

This is complicated.

I gave my mother a painting of sunflowers for mother's day 2010.

My mother used to walk by the painting at her best friend's house in Monterey. Her best friend was an older fabulous painter, whose mother used to be a New York socialite in the 1920s, who once sold off a block of Manhattan to throw a party. I was 20 and it was the most expensive thing I ever bought, even with the family discount. Pre-video call, she called me when she received it, the shock and joy in her voice, still burns in my memory. After she died, I only had two days to pack up her two-bedroom condo. As her body burned, I was quickly and efficiently organising and throwing away things. Numb, numb, numb. So Lonely. So quiet. And then there it was. The sunflower painting sitting next to her bed, not even hung yet. It's weird to give a gift and receive it in this way. For the first time in two days, I feel my heartstrings start to play like a violin. Small and high. I see a flash of her laughing in her best friend's garden, with the sunflowers behind her, slowly turning towards her. I slip the painting into my backpack, grab her medicine cards and rings and walk away. I tell this story today because a girl was crying in the back of the bus on our way home from Florence. She tells me this story had affected her the other day. That she had bought a painting in Florence for her mom and not one for herself. Because now she understood one day it would belong to her. A gift for the generations. Her Girasole.

MELISSA DAVID

6th july, 2022

today was immensely exciting, we explored Florence! i think the ambience of it is quite different from tuscany. the place was so lively, and there was much more to see. i love the rows of shops, and how it felt like walking in an outdoor museum of sorts. it started to rain somewhere along the way, but i love that we just didn't stop. back home, the first instinct after feeling raindrops on your skin is to seek shelter. that's how we've been conditioned to react.

i haven't taken a walk in drizzling rain in a long, long time. one of the little, simple things in life that i'll miss.

映月

KAITLYN YÍNG YUÉ

July 7th

Montecatini Alto

How do I sum up today in only a page or two? It's late and I'm exhausted, but in the best possible way. This morning, I taught three impromptu workshops— and of course I was a little worried that no one would show— but I was worried for nothing. I should have known! They all showed up! I could have cried right there, to be honest. Knowing these poets truly care what I have to say and what I have to share— I feel like the luckiest person in the world.

During my oracle poetry lesson, I chose a card for each of them and told them the meanings. They listened intently. Our group card was "Dreamtime/ Creation" which couldn't have been more fitting! While I was wrapping up— Jen, Denae, and Mel returned with tattoos! In my handwriting! They had actually done it— they all got matching tattoos! "You're with us forever," Mel said. I'm still smiling. My darling sunflowers.

Afterwards, I took a little solo detour to photograph the Terme and have a moment to myself to soak it all in and reflect. After I wrote a poem for one of my upcoming books, I met them in the park for a lovely picnic (that one very persistent bee tried to sabotage). Then we all gathered once more to visit the tiny town on top of the hill called Montecatini Alto.

After watching the sun set over the Tuscan hills, making a new little cat friend, and toasting champagne & reading poetry aloud to each other— a massive storm hit. That didn't slow us down. We danced in the rain, Catherine requested Whitney Houston from the restaurant (who could say no to her?), Mel sang to a couple inside the bar, we helped some of the restaurants bring in chair cushions & table settings (we were already soaked!), we laughed, we cheered, we lived every moment to it's fullest.

R. CLIFT

July 7

THIS DAY WAS THE DEFINITION OF SPONTANEOUS. WE HAD ARRANGED THE activity for the day to happen on the following- so we were left with the whole of the day free in Montecatini Terme. This avoided a bus ride five hours in total in a single day, which we all agree was too much.

Rachel planned— on the fly— three optional workshops. Creating a Healthy Relationship with Social Media, Self Publishing 101, and Basics of Oracle and Street Poetry. She wasn't sure who all would come but it turned out— everyone did. After the morning apart the workshops began in the atrium and were just as much chatting and sharing ideas about poetry, business, and inspiration as it was a 'class'. We all just wanted to spend the afternoon together— no matter the activity. Jen even arrived mid-workshop with her first tattoo ever— the word girasole in Rachel's handwriting.

We moved out to the veranda when the day grew fine and clustered around a long wicker and glass table under a large tree. Rachel did Oracle Poetry demonstrations as a few people ate takeaway from a spot nearby or painted with watercolors at the opposite end of the table with me. It was a moment in time entirely suspended in the present. No worries of the past or future. Before we knew it— almost four hours had passed.

We branched off before dinner— a few were going to get another tattoo. Rachel ran off for half an hour with her camera to photograph the Terme so I planned to grab a picnic for us from a market nearby. Some travelers went to investigate a cute restaurant, but when I opened the invitation to the rest— to my joy— quite a few joined me.

I introduced them to my love of Italian grocery stores. Mostly, a lot of my favorite foods are Italian so there's an advantage. But also— the produce is so fresh and affordable it's like it just came from the garden. We separated and ended up with a collective bundle of prosciutto, plums, focaccia, provolone, berries, olives, octopus, melon, chocolates, and pastries. We may have gone overboard a bit but Italian markets can have that effect.

We happily took our spoils a short walk to the large open fields of the park and set out a couple blankets on the grass. Rachel joined us and we played music over our phones, talked, and passed around foods both familiar and new.

The sun moved slowly towards the horizon as we got messages to meet up with the rest of the group on the train to go up the mountain. As luck would

XIV

have it, we found them on the walk there, and all arrived at the funicolare just before it was about to set off.

The little train was a single red car with a black roof and three large doors opening to one side. Huge windows with no glass adorned both sides. There were three indoor cabins and an outdoor platform at the back. Eight passengers could occupy each space so we piled in with strangers and the train began its laborious climb to Montecatini Alto. We were headed to the old medieval section of the town as we were told it could not be missed.

We arrived and alighted to the overlook just as the blazing orange sun sent almost solid rays of light across the town below. The sky was gigantic—yellow and pink. We stood in awe, took photos, and wrote poetry. A small pageant was in the works to reenact the iconic "flying" scene from Titanic when Mel appeared from a little side street and told us to go find Jen.

Not realizing they had snuck off in the first place, we wound our way through the tiny alleys and discovered her at a long wooden table under a canopy of flowers and lights.

"I found us a table," she said with a smile.

It was a gorgeous spot at the edge of a small square surrounded by restaurants. Families and couples milled about as we all sat down to a spread of snacks and rosé wine.

We shared poems that had been written through the week and reveled in the magic that unfolded. As we were finishing the wine it began to rain. Slowly at first, so naturally a few of our group ran out to dance in the square to the loud music emanating from the nearby restaurant. Catherine asked the waiters very nicely and they even played *Dance With Somebody* for us. We all joined in and other families got up from their tables to dance with us. Eventually, however, umbrellas began to fly on the wind and we took cover with many others in the tiny bar area of *La Rughetta*. The rain and lightning were so strong we were stuck and sure the train wouldn't be running. What were we to do?

A toast and a song, of course. We took little paper cups and passed around a bottle of white wine, to everyone gathered, and cheered to the rain and the moon and all of us. Mel sang a song and the other patrons were already smiling along. The room went from anxious to joyful as we made quite a few new friends from Ireland and Germany.

Eventually the rain subsided and we left that little place at the top of the mountain still humming and singing. We shined together like the stars that night, the entire walk home.

XV

Am I a Poet?

Who in the world am I?

am I the quiet and proper academic?
the red-haired girl claiming to be an artist?
a writer trying to find her way?
am I a daughter with no home?
or a wanderer who must find joy in roaming?

I want to line the pieces up
and turn the kaleidoscope of me
until there's just
one face—
one identity—
looking back

maybe that
will really be me

- Leigh

AND I WILL KEEP YOU TUCKED AWAY

LIKE SCRAPS OF PAPER AND PRESSED FLOWERS

GILDED WITH GOLD AND GREEN AND WHITE

COLLECTED ON RAINY DAYS BETWEEN THE PAGES OF

MY NOTEBOOK THAT HASN'T SEEN THE LIGHT OF DAY IN YEARS

WHOSE LEATHER BINDING IS STAINED FROM

SPILLED TEA AND ALL MY TEARS

THAT CRY *"WHAT IF?"*

AND ARE ANSWERED WITH, *"WHAT NOW?"*

AND FALL TOO SHORT TO STAND UP TALL

AND SIT SO QUIETLY ON A SHELF

WITH THE REST OF MY DAYDREAMS.

FREYDIS LOVA

Ink

Waiting for the ink to dry,
From where your poetry
now rests on my chest.
She is the creator,
The tattoo artist,
Attaching herself to you,
As if she's always been there.

– Mel

Mel

to turn towards the sun

All our tattoos are
in Rachel's handwriting!

to turn towards the sun

Denae

Malena

Girasole

In a field of wildflowers
You are a single sunflower
Standing taller than the rest
Unafraid to open your petals
I want to always remember you this way –
Always turning towards the sun

– Jen

Lisa, the tattoo artist
in Montecatini Terme
@liv.needles

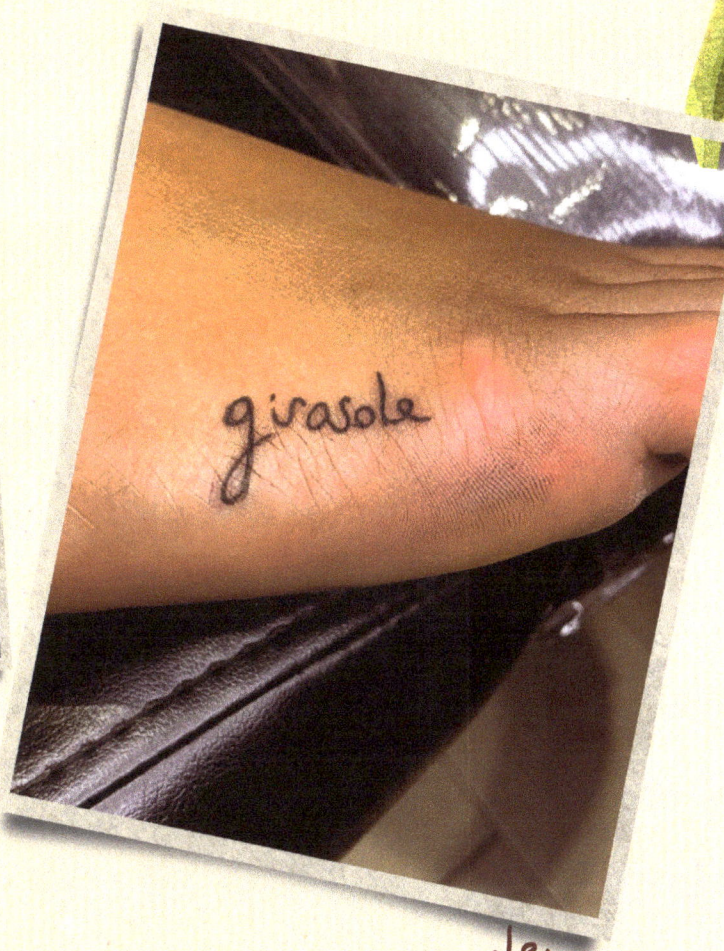

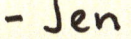

Jen

for rachel, our earthly yet ethereal muse, and friend.

***

she's the kind that lets tears fall,
as words rushes to spill out from her.
she's the kind to pull you up when you trip,
fussing over your lightly scraped knees
and giving you the warmest embrace.

while she's very much made of this earth
and all of nature's innermost feelings,
i sincerely believe that
she's a physical manifestation of a blue star
picked from the darkest night sky,
here to walk these flowered paths with us
and be a guiding light.

i thank the stars and the moon
that she's here with us
for this moment in time.
i thank the stars and the moon
that most of all,
she's here for her heart.

KAITLYN YÍNG YUÈ

The First Line

Sometimes all you have is the first line,
the first thought on the page.
You have to trust when and only when you write it,
the second and third will follow.

The first line you write can seem like the most daunting time
because the world is asking you *"how will this poem end?"*

God knows all you have is that first line
and to not write that first line would be a sin.

You can talk about your great idea,
but nothing exists until you write
that first line.

CATHERINE PITTS

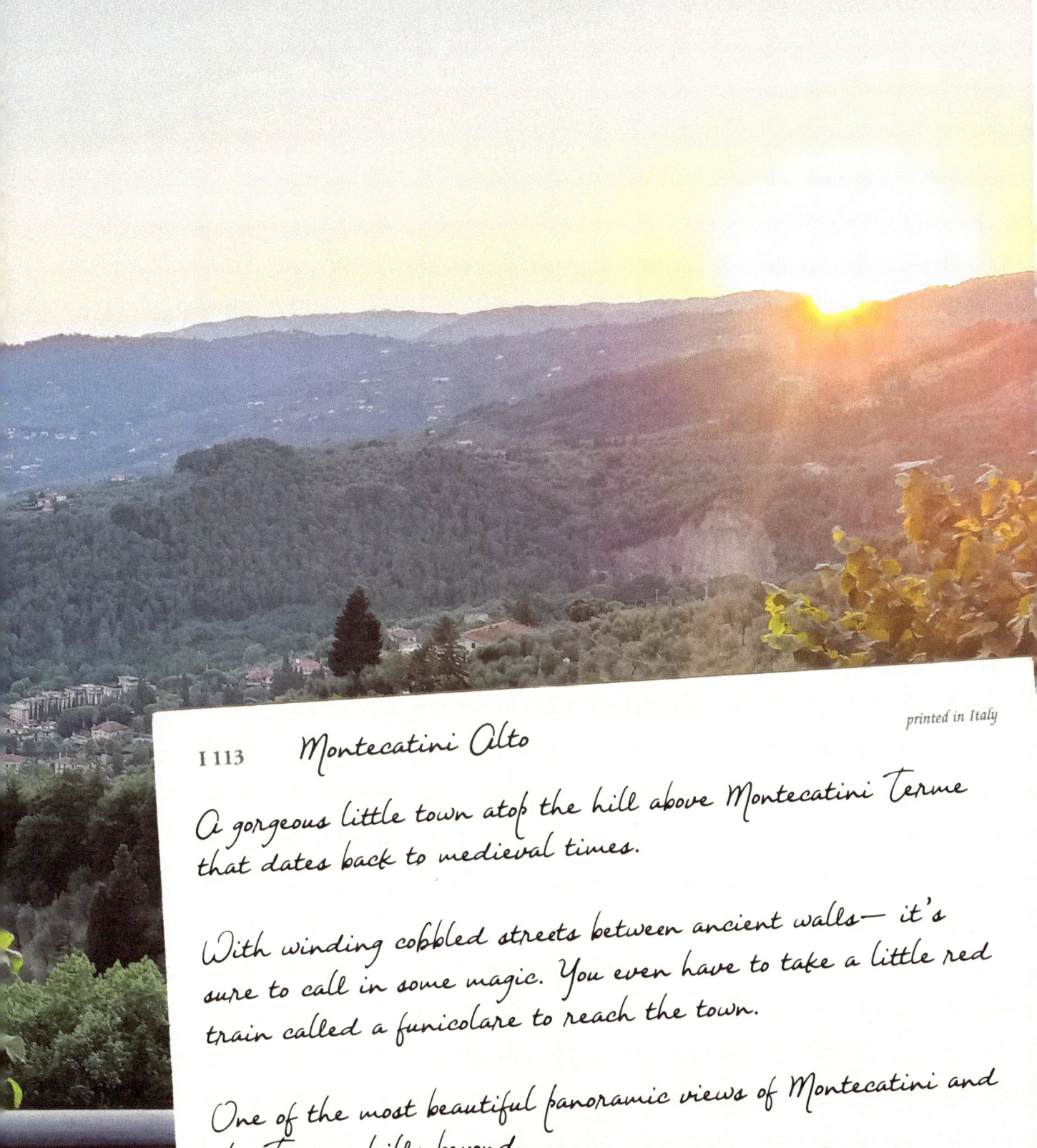

printed in Italy

I 113 Montecatini Alto

A gorgeous little town atop the hill above Montecatini Terme that dates back to medieval times.

With winding cobbled streets between ancient walls— it's sure to call in some magic. You even have to take a little red train called a funicolare to reach the town.

One of the most beautiful panoramic views of Montecatini and the Tuscan hills beyond.

funiculì, funiculà

little red gigia chugs along
  her track up the side
of the mountain
  just as she always has
since 1898, passing gigio
  where the track splits
in two, reconjoining
  after gigio's passengers
wave to us as they descend.
  from where we stand
at the back of the funicular,
  the mountains recede
in the twilight, fringed by the
  nearing dusk's aura.

at the top, the man running
  the funicular whistles
the song looping in my head:

funiculì, funiculà, funiculì,
  funiculà, 'ncoppa
jamme jà funiculì, funiculà!

FUNICOLARE MONTECATINI s.r.l.
Viale Diaz, 22
51016 Montecatini Terme (PT)
P. IVA 00837260470

€7
ANDATA - RITORNO
HIN UND ZURÜCK
ROUND TRIP
ALLER - RETOUR
IDA Y VUELTA

N⁰   343

EMMA CONLON

Have you known the strength in silence?
The true strength,
that beats in sync with
a heart that had been so hurt
you can't help but stand in awe
and wonder how it
can be filled with selfless love for so many?
You have if you have met her.
Looked into her eyes.
Heard her laugh
and held her hand
as she comforts you while you cry.
She is the calm, not after,
but during the storm.
And you will never have to
board your windows
or hide from her.

afterglow

the silhouettes of birds that darken the dwindling sky
spread shadowy wings across the clouds, light flecks
of spilled ink flicked haphazardly by some giant quill
dribbling from the freshly dipped point across
the gradient sky. the sun's blush leaves the heavens
flushed with brilliant saffrons, apricots and tangerines;
the puffy clouds mottling the horizon, drifting
mauvy-indigo and tinged with a gilded rose where
the slinking sunbeams still can breach, tumbling
and giddy. with her last breaths, the dying sun hoists
fiery tendrils over craggy mountains. she takes her
final bow after a long day's performance—we applaud.
she dips her golden head behind those resting giants,
slumbering in the haze of cornflowers and cobalts,
solemn in their vow of timeless watch over this valley.
the hills of forests are tinged blue as the sunlight trickles
away like sand through an hourglass—they blend
noiselessly into the vast expanse of clouds, now dawdling
low along the aureole of dimming gold. the afterglow
lingers, loiters, leeches—drains from the sky, concealing
the terraced rows of terracotta houses in silky dark.

EMMA CONLON

laura reads a poem

and the thunder rolls in applause / and your heart swells and threatens to overflow in your chest / and you can barely contain your unbridled joy / and you feel a lovely warmth wash over every inch of your skin / and you wish you could hold this moment in your hands forever / and you sip rosé as you listen to each verse / and you sigh, dreamy with the thick it, of all this *delight* / and all this *serendipity* / and all this *understanding* / and you know something in you has shifted / and you know nothing is the same as it was.

laura reads her poems
/ and the sky cracks open in answer.

EMMA CONLON

Laura painted a sunflower for each of our travelers to take home with them!

Old Town (Me)

it's easy
to be happy
in a beautiful place
pink skies
blue mountains
palms swaying
delicate clouds
that could be continents
or castles in the air
but I need to find this
place
inside my beating chest
where my swirling mind
can come back to the
beauty
and the stillness
in me

LEIGH FISHER

203

XI.

As nymphs all gather to dance in the rain,
and two strangers wander,
they're completely in awe
while they sway.
A siren sings to voyagers
biding them to come hither.
To join in our joyous day.

She's mystic. She's lightning.
She's the one who proudly taught us
it was alright to fill this space.
Synced with thunder and rain,
adventurers and vagabonds
cheer her praise.
They laugh and cry as
the moonlight embraced
each emotion they gave.

Scan to listen to the
siren song

CAS McDOWELL

Love is like lighting, all have heard of it,
some say they've seen it,
but few have ever been struck by it

J.S.

Landmine

Today I believe in magic, completely, utterly, unapologetically. My essence is so one with the pulsation of the universe, I feel like I'm on another plane, another dimension. She said I was lightning and then there it was. Sparkling down on me. They have started writing poems about me, did you hear? But more importantly, they have started reading their own pieces, which means more than anything. I step into what they think is a landmine field, only to show them it's just the ground. The same ground they learned to walk on so many years ago. I press into the lightning too much and the wind starts to make it all break. I say hello and goodbye to the moon, as we tuck into our little bar on the hill. I sing for her, her works freshly inked on my heart. She stands in the back observing, leading from the back like a wolf. As we head home a flower is handed through a window. A final offering on a perfect unexplainable, cosmic, fateful day. Today I know there is magic.

MELISSA DAVID

in defense of wandering

to be lost is to be free.
"lost" led me to the
marble arches
who kindly whispered
a few of the secrets
they've collected
through the centuries.
"lost" led me to paintings
of worlds thus far
unknown to me
and sculptures birthed
from earthen treasures.
"lost" led me to gardens
so lush, so mystifying,
so unscathed by
the weary world
you may just lay down
roots of your own.
it led me to joys beyond
my flawed imagination.
it led me to you.

EMMA CONLON

We leave not to come back
to who we once were,
but to integrate our true essence
into the potential we can be

— Denae Terese

there are so many things
I don't let myself feel
or confess
upon the page

and I really believed
just a few honest words
whispered here and there
were enough

but it's not enough for me
and I'm not a betting girl
but I'd wager
it's not enough for you either

Brunello

Tell me

Tell me that you love me,
Even if it hurts,
Even if there is no hope.
Just hold me for this moment,
And tell me you love me.

Sit

I love how close we are,
I love that out of everywhere,
You chose to sit next to me.

MELISSA DAVID

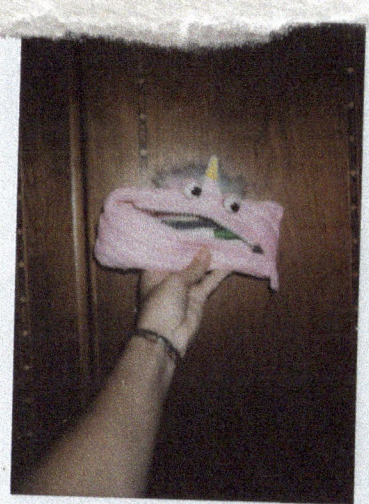

Picture

I'm missing a picture.
A picture of you loving me,
Was it real?
Or was it just a painting
I imagined?

MELISSA DAVID

211

Atop this mountain I stand
having travelled a trail so few
have ever found and fewer still have
followed. I see now
that it was the rough rocks and ridges
of this path that made me into the
man capable of climbing it.
Fall as I did, abandoned as I felt,
and beaten as I am. Here I finally
stand amongst souls of the same,
staring down upon the stars below.

J.S.

J.S.

XII.

You're in a field of wildflowers.
Before you stood isolated.

One fall stripped your seeds away.
The wind carried you out to sea.

Winter came. You lied dormant.
Curious when you'd wake.

By Spring, you knew this place
Would gift a life filled
With beauty and truth.

You're in a field of wildflowers.
You are not alone.
The wind had called and
Introduced each one to you.
Their story. Their life.
Their beauty. Their pain.

You're in a field of wildflowers.
My darling, you are not alone.

CAS McDOWELL

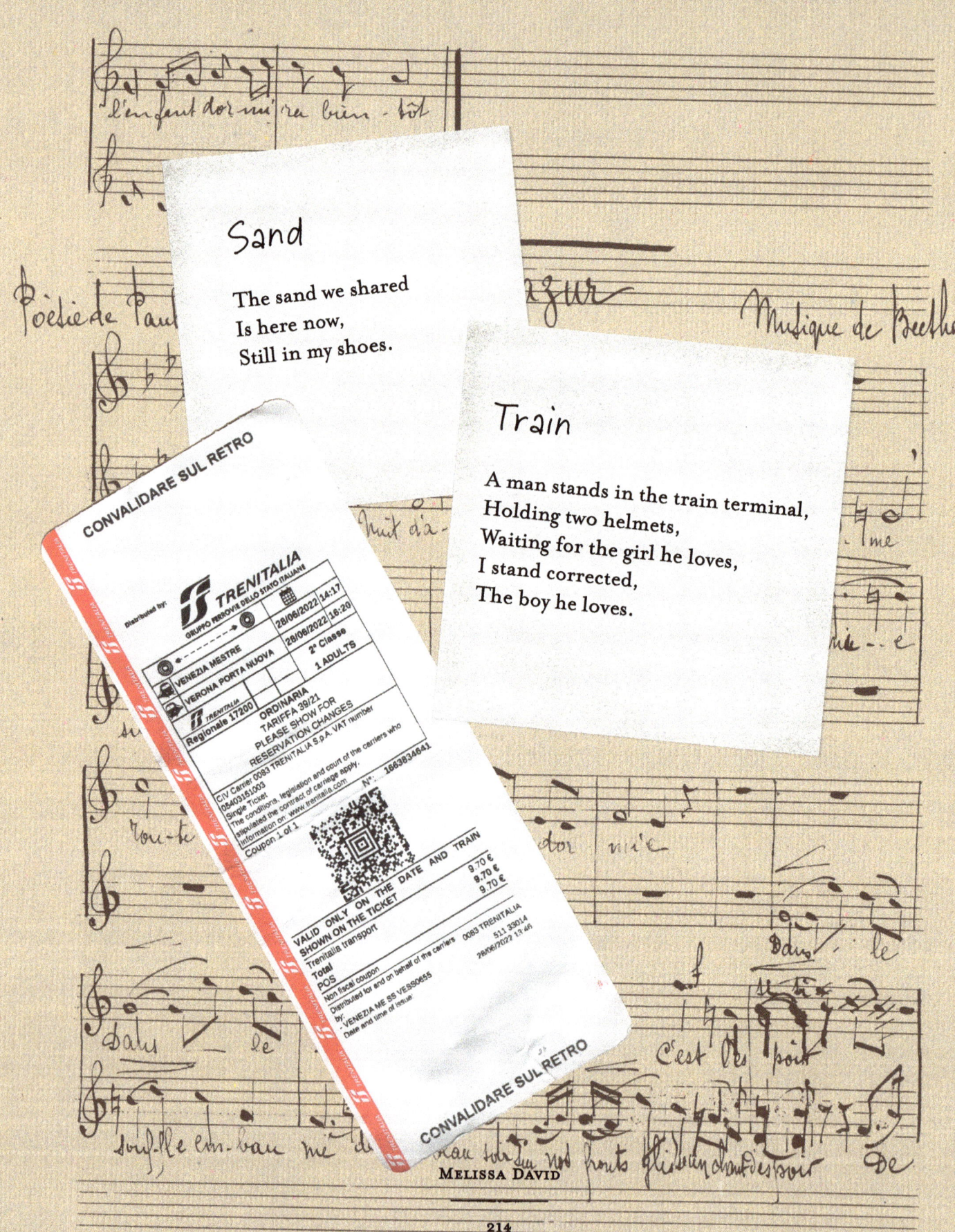

Sand

The sand we shared
Is here now,
Still in my shoes.

Train

A man stands in the train terminal,
Holding two helmets,
Waiting for the girl he loves,
I stand corrected,
The boy he loves.

MELISSA DAVID

alone again (practically)

without my noticing,
        the laughter
of my companions has
        slid away,
growing fainter as I write,
        raging against
the dying light, helping
        the poem
fight its way into being.
        the mountains,
my sole companions,
        at least until
the little red funicular
        returns
with more who hunger
        for this view
as I do. the milky dusk
        has cooled
to a smoldering ember,
        singeing the skyline—
cinders & ash, charcoal & soot.
        one by one,
pinpricks of light burst
        into being
(not a fight, like the poem,
        but a birth)
across the drowsy town
        below. I watch
as they flare like flint-strikes
        in sequenced
procession, the guiding lights
        we follow,
a beacon to call us home.

EMMA CONLON

There is a sweetness in her smile
that has also known grief
and pain that would tear a soul to shreds
but she has taken the ribbons
of broken hearts and set aside dreams
and wrapped up her tomorrows
with wishes and warm hugs
that mirror a tuscan sunrise
and given them to the souls
she has stitched together
from the farthest points of the earth,
making the globe feel
just a little bit smaller -
and how wonderful is that,
that she can smile
and we can feel her embrace
from anywhere in the world?

FREYDIS LOVA

216

longing in any other language

I miss you with such a deep longing
that it overflows in my chest, the rising
yearning, the wild pressure of it
knocking the air from my lungs.
every tendon, every vein, each thin filament
aches for you, aches with the grief
of separation, despite its brevity.
my body reminds me I cannot bear
to be without you.

      the open wound of it.
the phantom ache that skulks about
the empty air beside me. your missing
presence does not haunt me, it pains me.

I am in the most beautiful place I've ever been
but the distance splits like a canyon,
splits me apart
      like an open wound.
whatever it is I am made of, be it soul or mind
or nothing more than electrical flesh, that
deep part in me yearns for you across
the atlantic.   can you hear her?
in the moments we are apart, I cannot ease
this ache. this yearning. every heartbeat
speaks your name. every breath empty
without the sound of your breathing
      beside me. perhaps
this is the kind of love all the greats
wrote about. the kind of love that
launches one thousand ships, hell,
one million ships. more.
      the kind of love
romeo and juliet died for in verona,
a few regions over, a few centuries back.

if this is the love great poets wrote of,
I cannot count myself among them.
my 24 years have not known virtuosic
visions. I'm no prodigy. but
      I'm doing the best I can.
      don't we all?

EMMA CONLON

———

*Freydis's photo of Emma reminded
me of "The Soul of the Rose" by
John William Waterhouse.
Art is life, life is art.*

— R.

218

What I wouldn't give
if not all of my tomorrows
for just a chance at one last today with her

J.S.

To the souls who have traveled with me, created with me, loved and lost and mourned with me — we are the breath of a renaissance that history may not know, but will change the world nonetheless.

— freydis lova

FREYDIS LOVA

I carry them with me
words gifted in secret
meant only for my heart
that I have heard in my dreams before
stepping onto this land
and looking into familiar eyes
for the first time.
My journals pages are torn
and worn and I am in awe
of how they do not tear
from the weight of the messages
that have been left, trusted, in my hands.
to the souls who traveled with me
created with me
loved and lost and mourned with me

We are the breaths of a renaissance
that history may not know
but will change the world
nonetheless.

FREYDIS LOVA

7th july, 2022

today, we had a free day from our schedule because as beautiful as Florence was, we were tired from a full day of being there. i personally don't think i've walked that much in 24 hours. even so, i guess poets and artists rest in a different way, because we decided to spend the day listening to rachel introducing us to a few things about poetry. watching everyone doing their own things while intently hearing her talk is a type of contentment i wish i could always have. i find myself doing that a lot on this retreat. excitement and awe are a given, but i've never felt so content in knowing i don't really need to do much else other than just exist. i went to sit by myself after a while, just listening to music, reading some pages of a book and watch the sunlight stream through the trees.

‡‡‡

oh... what a night to remember. if my memories could exist out of my being, i'd keep tonight in a reel of film

and replay it as often as i can. it's the kind of memory
that you already know you'll miss dearly as the moments
are being made. we decided to go up to Montecatini Alto
for the evening, and stayed for dinner. the view overlooking
the stretch of Tuscany, mountain lines and endless sky was
simply mesmerising.

we saw the lightning flash before we felt the rain. our feet
moved before we heard the music. tonight, we danced until
the rain was summoned and we continued anyway. dancing
in the rain is such a movie thing to do, but it happened
tonight and it was absolutely magical. storms and the
excitement of the night only fueled us, and we were sung to
and toasted and loved. with our hearts on our rain soaked
sleeves, we were there.

KAITLYN YÍNG YUÉ

July 8th

Brunello Winery
&
Back to Rome

It's hard to believe this week is already coming to an end. I've barely slept all week— between excitement and lesson planning and exploring— there's been no time for sleep! I'm so tired, but more than that, so overwhelmingly happy. I didn't know I could be this happy.

Catherine pointed out that there are eleven blooms on my 'super sunflower' back home and eleven travelers here. That sunflower began blooming the day we left for Italy. This is fate. This is destiny. I am witnessing my destiny.

Here I am. At the beginning of a new chapter— a new life. One where I can cry in front of strangers and give them a safe place to create. One where we smile— "even in the winter— even in the rain." A daydream. A.S.J. Tessimond's 'Daydream' come to life.

These people are magic— this trip is cosmic. This has shown me my purpose in life so clearly. To bring people together, to show them the world, to be inspired, and to leave a little brighter than when we arrived. What an honor it is to know them, what a privilege it has been to be their teacher. I hope I never forget this feeling.

My sunflower with eleven blooms!

Fattoria dei Barbi
Montalcino

stayed the same
that's okay
...ned into a world of bi...

...nknown & unfamiliar, but a ...
...nd all ...
...e been
...mily
...family
...s me blush and sm...

everyone to see
in your presence
holds me deep
...g time, Peace.
...t screams!

July 8

Our last day. We spent much of it refusing to admit it, stamping our feet into the present moment like children and refusing any sadness. Not yet. We still had a whole day.

The first couple hours were spent on the bus, driving through sunflower fields, towards Rome. We had started to call each other, by now, *my sunflowers.* Everything was so different from the last time we drove these roads only a week before. Then, it had been new— everyone was just meeting— feeling separated from Italy and each other. But now— there were sunflowers outside and in. We moved to sit together, braided hair, and shared chocolates. It was so comfortable, the warm Italian sun and the air— full and sweet with flowering jasmine, must have worked itself deep into our lungs and souls. We turned towards the sun. Towards each other.

Our first stop was a Brunello Winery for our last workshop. It was a little complex of pale orange buildings with red tiled roofs nestled close together in the center of a large vineyard. We sat together at a stone table under a grove of chestnut trees.

Everyone wrote exquisite-corpse poems together, voices mingling on paper and within the sizzling leaves above. After a wine tasting- deep red wine- we returned to our drive and laughed together the whole way to Rome.
Our farewell dinner was none other than the classic pizza Margherita. We read poems for Federica and said goodbye in the hotel lobby in the same green and gold corner where we first said hello. Then it was just us. Thirteen people who were not ready to leave each other yet.

So— we didn't.

We walked together until we stumbled upon an overlook of the city in Villa Borghese and read aloud the poems we wrote together that day. We

XVI

counted stars and tried not to slip on marble steps— clutching each other's hands as if we might float away once parted. Through Piazza del Popolo, where J.S. appeared with a huge bunch of roses and handed them out with a smile as we laughed in astonishment.

Each poem read, painting shared, gift bestowed— we were reaching out to each other as the moments passed and pulled us closer to goodbye. It grew late and we ignored the time. Got gelato by the Spanish Steps, found a hidden courtyard and watched the people dancing there, and finally— ended at the Trevi Fountain. *Of course.*

It was the same. Clear swaths of water rushing over stone figures into the turquoise basin below. Crowds and proposals and voices so loud you could hardly think. Trevi was constant, but it felt different than before. We had changed.

The ghosts of our first visit occupied the corner on the right, throwing in coins and eliciting cheers from strangers, wishing to return. I could hear the laughter- it was still with me, after all. For just a few more moments.

I made a different wish that night on our long walk back and during our reluctant farewells. That we would meet again, under some distant sun, and fall easily into each other's company, to create new art and memories— and tell stories of the time we spent together, one bright July, in Italy.

XVII

printed in Italy

I 113

Brunello Winery – Fattoria dei Barbi, Montalcino

The Colombini family, who have owned land in Montalcino since 1532, have cared for and operated the winery since the 18th century. They are producers of the famous Brunello– an award-winning wine beloved across the world.

Both pioneers in wine tourism and keepers of tradition, the Fatttoria dei Barbi is a cornerstone of wine in Italy.

Edizioni D'Arte I.F.I. Firenze
Riproduzione vietata

Art & Poetry Workshop Three

you've stayed the same
And that's okay
i transitioned into a world of bidets and
                                    yoni steams,
a world unknown & unfamiliar, but a world where
I have found
a home. my heart has finally found all of you, artists
& poets.
without knowing it, I think I have been searching
for you all my life. Emma

        friends that feel like family
        a breeze that feels eerily familiar
    everything about you makes me blush and smile

MiL.
    You look at me
    And I wonder if it is plain for everyone to see
    The strength that grows in me in your presence
    Fills me with endless energy. It holds me deep
    with, for the first time in a long time, Peace.
    Don't forget me, my romantic heart screams!
    For I fear the memory of you will slip the same way
    It leaves me to question, was it ever real if it can fade away?

                                            easily
    No love is the same and it's yours my heart longs for Oh Denae

    I can't help but to reach in and explore your past sorrows
    ask if i can hold your heart safely in my hands
    and know the preciousness of your love K.C

may we be carried away on a sea of pure moonlight — as if simply
          existing, living & being in this moment finally be enough.
                                                    can

I was alive in this dream yet dying when awake

Searching so long through the darkest days of night —
I wonder where you are my long lost love I have yet to meet

"Ja Lune", I call, "bring them home to me."
The planets and stars sympathize for us feeling
this distance so far between.
You sitting in silence, or thinking in solitude. Though I hope these
calls forever reach you.
I CM
And yet, a part of my heart hopes they remain
unsung melodies between our drifting souls —
forever a dream buried between constellations.   freydis

        we met once upon a time waltzing among
                    the stars

[KR]   a former ~~shooting~~ star family

      then we dissapeared into a̶ black hole abyss
   a place beyond the only world we've known.
   still there is a quiet beauty in the darkness,
 a voiceless hope that calls out to us from all
    this dark. emma
                                        will again
       A new day will rise, And the sun will shine
P   There's beaty in forever and there's beauty in goodbye.
    In this I'll stand, my heart forever changed, by this old land.

      The treasured memories I've made
Mil   The new people I now call my own, my friends
      I carry them all with me into this new future

   Into this new me. Full of peace and memories, full of you adore
   Forever seems like such a long time when you break it down to 3.
Marly "Three magical days of wonder", the moon and rain screams,
              all of
       echoing through time ~~itself~~ — until the universe collapses in on itself,
                                        and our poetry is all that remains.

moments swarm past my eyes as fleeting as the day turns to night
i try to stitch every memory into my veins,   DH *Denae*
but the thread never seems to stay tight

even as i try to hold on to it
                from
it slips ˄ my fingers
and something in me breaks loose   K-C
like a floodgate chattering open into a hurricane
a being overflowing from my heart, around my neck,
and finally rushing over my head

The waves keep crashing. The tide is pulling me in.
I'm grasping for breath, and feel that bone chill sink deep.
under I fall, but its not terrifying. It's quiet, peaceful and calm. CM
Just as you are to me for the those dark days when
                       isn't   even
the silence is quiet, the air isn't in my lungs, and ho
hope isn't in my heart there you are for me, all I will ever need

and still, selfishly, I long for more—
to hold you in my arms and feel you breathe in my embrace,
but in my heart you will stay with all of the other ghosts.   freydis
your voice forever intertwined with mine
ⓐ I couldn't forget you even if I tried
For even the strawberries remind me of your cheeks

How lucky am I
Mil You are everywhere I turn
     And I love this world all the more for the pieces of you
     I see in it. And when you look into my eyes, you can tell
     I've never ~~ever~~ cared for goodbyes—so instead you take my hand,
           and with a small smile, you whisper, "Until we meet again." Mabel

A Letter To Us

(each line was inspired by someone in the group)

You led us here with infinite grace,
taught us new art,
bought us gifts,
and sang.

You read us your poems of waves and rain,
and taught us "girasole" was a forever thing.

You told us stories of a foreign land,
displayed boldness,
and reminded me of the beauty of new friends.

Your laughter filled the room,
as your art filled my heart.

Your courage paved the way,
and your determination and consistency
got us from place to place.

In the end - you left us all forever changed.

CATHERINE PITTS

MALENA GRACE

235

MALENA GRACE

236

XIII.

These familiar faces I never want to leave.
It was only day one and it was as if we'd always known.

CAS MCDOWELL

For Mel

She's an expander
Elastic
A rubber band around your heart
Her poetry is the kind I want to read
Witty and playful
Filled with sarcastic and dry one liners
"Don't forget to bring your extra panties"
She'd call out
As we walked out the door to adventure together
It was like we'd known each other forever
The day I met her -
She was walking straight out of a confessional
As she waved bye to the priest
And twirled down the front of that church's steps
One night
Lightning striked across the sky behind her
From that moment-on she electrified strangers
She often held out her hand to meet mine
And gave it a gentle squeeze
A quiet agreement of a newfound lifelong friendship
Sealed in silence between two strangers
The center of an intricate web
A singer
The best kind gift giver
Eighteen hundred copy of hamlet for one and eighteen carat gold for another
Always running towards the music
Then she'll sing and draw you in
Finding lifeless women and pulling them up to dance alongside her
She keeps all of her tattoos hidden between her hips and her tits
Keeping foresight on all her political dreams
A self-made millionaire yet, you'd never know it
I even watched her pull money out of the sky one time
I often look at her and think,
"That girl
Her -
Reflecting back forgotten parts of me,
She has something I need"

JENNIFER GELLOCK

238

Last night

Last night on the top of a Tuscan mountain,
We got stuck in a bar as the storm raged by.
I sang for strangers and we passed the time.

Sobriety

Sobriety can be lonely.
Sobriety can be isolating.
But as I sit outside
In the Tuscan air alone
With my meats and cheeses,
I just feel brave.
My demons are quiet now, sleeping.
Every day I say no,
I become a little stronger.
I don't mind the isolation.
I never feel lonely anymore.

MELISSA DAVID

i wish you were here with me.
oh, how great would it be
to walk these cobblestoned streets
together,
to laugh and hold hands under
rome's dimmed streetlights,
and gaze at each other
until the stars are jealous.

when we were young,
we used to dream
in brightly lit tents,
snuggled under blankets
with fits of giggles,
waiting to burst out
from our lungs.

oh, how great would it be
to have you here with me,
so i can love you endlessly.

KAITLYN YÍNG YUÉ

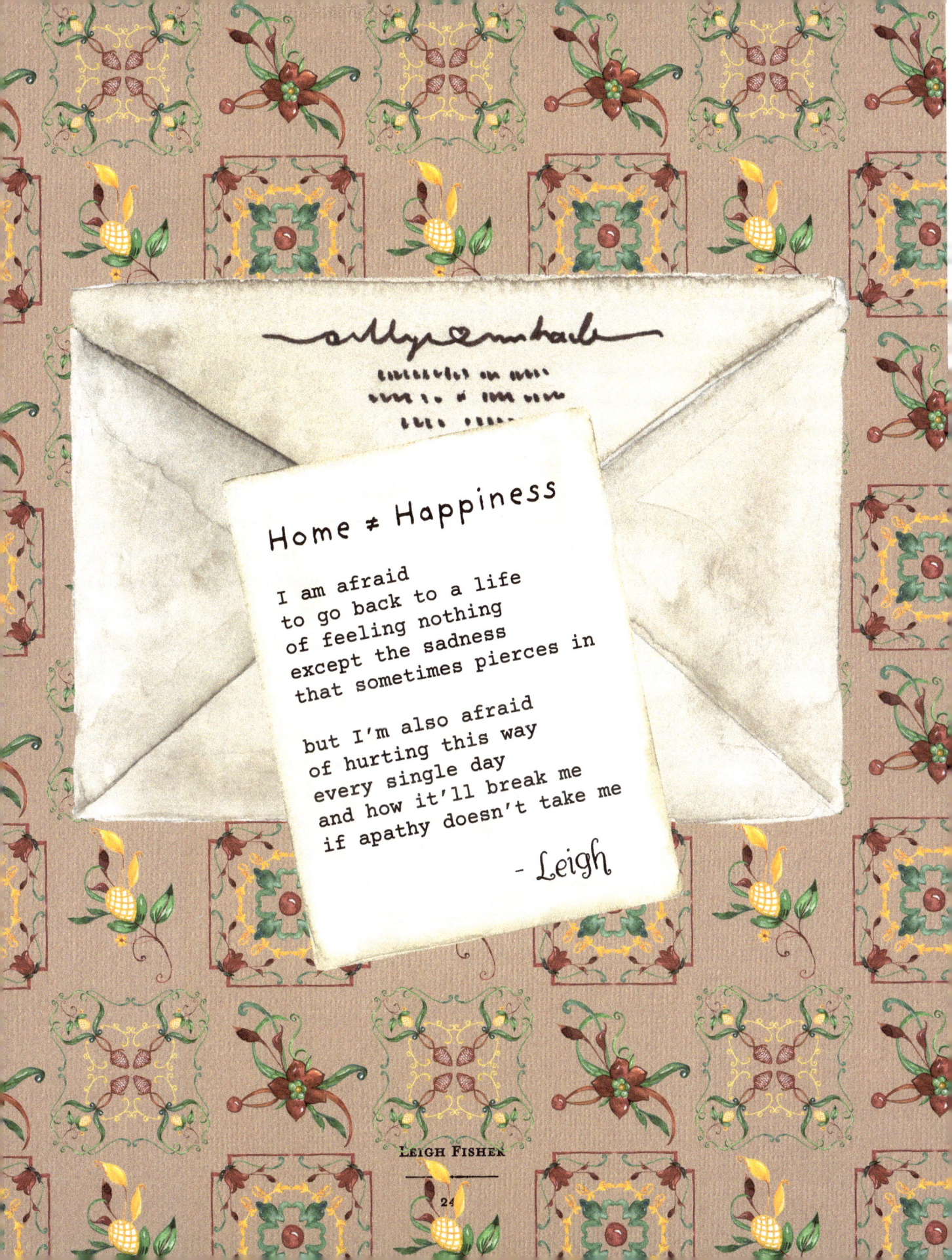

Home ≠ Happiness

I am afraid
to go back to a life
of feeling nothing
except the sadness
that sometimes pierces in

but I'm also afraid
of hurting this way
every single day
and how it'll break me
if apathy doesn't take me

- Leigh

I'm hungry now, I realise.
As a child, I wasn't fed, and instead
I filled the hunger with visions of feasts I'd one day eat.
But the lack of substance made me grow accustomed to it.
I don't need that much I'd say.

Years later I was tortured with the taste of sweets being held over me.
If I'm a good girl, a good wife, they will give me another taste.
Years of control of my intake of food to the point where I didn't care anymore for these sweets. I left this restaurant, giving it a poor review, as it was not the restaurant advertised online as much as it tried.

Finally some food. Some self-indulgence of what others see as a basic necessity of life.
Fattened and self-reliant I learn what it's like to walk around not famished.

I can feed other people now, I can see like no other when someone is hungry.
I am satisfied with myself peacefully sitting and drinking my tea.
The wind picks up.
What's that smell?
Mmmm do you smell that, I ask the breeze.
As soon as it blows through my nostrils it is gone.
Hmmmm, never mind then.
I gather a feast for my friends in my new estate, built by yours truly. Gas oven, Moroccan counter tops, with a sink large enough to wash a turkey or a fat baby.
Mid-meal I head to the kitchen to grab another bottle of wine as my friends laugh, bellies full, from the indoor/outdoor dining room.
A whiff of the smell again stops me mid-cork pop.
I swivel quickly this time to locate the source.
There it is! in the oven, right in my kitchen where it's been the entire time.
I slowly walk up to it afraid it might disappear again.
I lower myself to the level of the glass and press my fingers to it slowly.
It's warm. With another whiff I'm frozen.

MELISSA DAVID

———

The oven light flashes.

Meat, potatoes, vegetables, spices, sauces dripping in a way that looks familiar yet completely new.

I excitingly try to open the oven door.

It's locked.

I try again to no avail.

It's not ready, a voice says.

But it looks and smells delicious, I say out loud.

It's not ready.

Realising I'm talking to my oven, I shake it off grab the half-corked wine and shake my head smiling as I walk back into the long wooden table surrounded by my friends.

I tell them about this delicious thing in my oven that only appears randomly, smells like heaven, but that it's not ready.

Months go buy. Other food starts to lose its taste. The memories of the smell from my kitchen make me do stupid things like lock my keys inside or miss a turn cause I'm day-dreaming about this meal.

Sometimes I just sit in front of the oven and wait to see if it appears.

One night the smell is so strong I can't sleep. I march into the kitchen and demand to know when it will be ready!

It says nothing but the oven light is on and I can smell it, so I settle for a seat in front of it.

You can have a taste in two weeks the voice says.

I'm not sure I'll make it that long without food I laugh.

Two weeks it says.

I wait, start to lose weight, start to feel the old patterns creep back into my body.

I can wait.

Two weeks, not a sound, not a peep. The food looks unchanged. I'm worried it's missing an ingredient, so I place random things outside the oven like a crazy person just in case.

I wait.

I'm past hungry now, just sitting in the quiet, delirious.

I dream of walking into a room and there is a buffet! Someone says, *oh thank god you're here,*

MELISSA DAVID

———

I have so much to share. I've gotten rid of the mold and put fresh fruit out just this morning. Please help me eat all this food! I laugh and open the door behind me, I also have a buffet! I've been collecting it over the last couple of years. Please join me and my friends and let's eat.
They say, can I bring my buffet?

Of course, I say as I explode in joy.

I come back to on the cold kitchen ground, I must have fallen asleep I think.
It's okay the voice says.
Go have your buffet, you're hungry, you need to eat.

But I've been waiting and you smell so good I say.

I'm not ready and I'll never be a buffet.

Exhausted I drag my hand one more time across the oven glass to feel the warmth.

I walk away from my kitchen and order my favourite takeout. I need to eat I think.
No more starving for anything anymore.

Time goes by, fattened and healthy, I eat.

Every once in a while when I'm hosting a dinner party, I get a whiff from the kitchen.
I smile to myself and think, it's still there, always there, just cooking away.

I refocus my attention on the cake in front of me that my best friend made
for my birthday.
They start to sing in perfect harmony and together we eat cake.

MELISSA DAVID
———————

Allerseelen

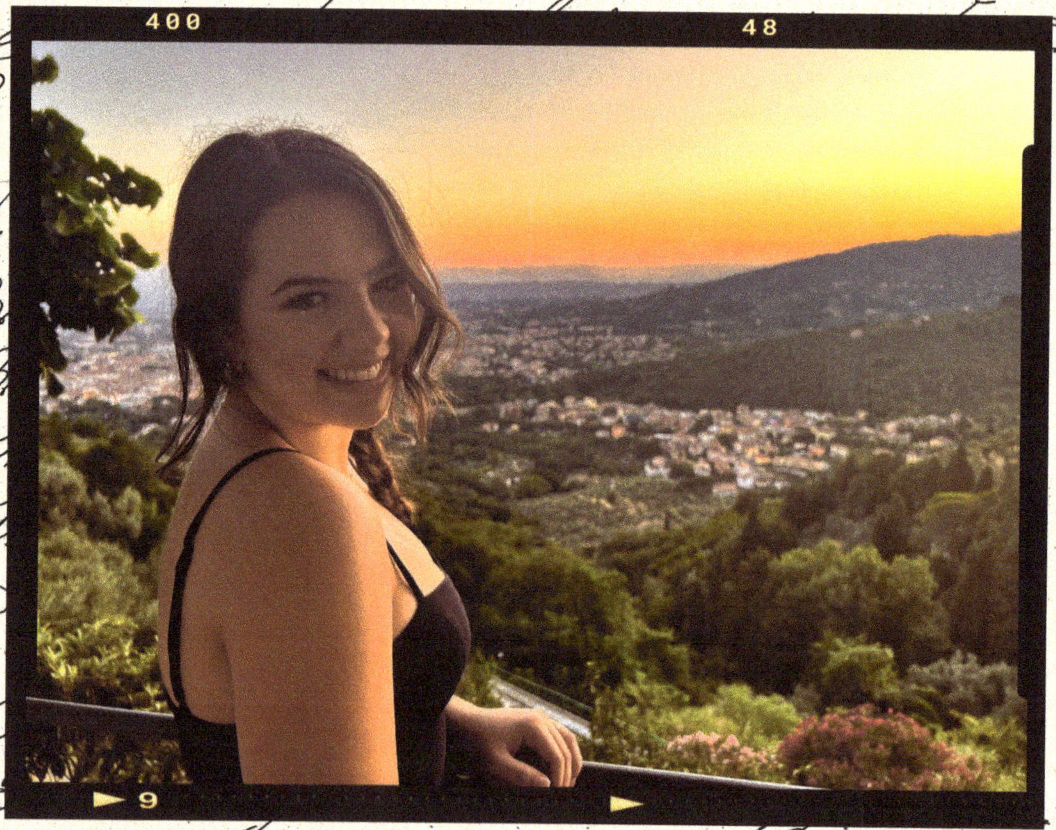

Cupid's Got Games

Cupid's arrows fly in front of me,
this way, that way,
like I'm living a romantic parody.

My mind won't let go,
it won't let me get hit by that stupid arrow.

And to be quite frank, I think this cupid has seen better days.
I mean have you seen the guys he brings my way?

C'mon, it's like he's preparing to retire.
Even my grandma knows he's a golden satire.

I like to imagine but then push forward strong.
It's time to pick up my own bow and arrow,
and decide what category of drama I want to call my own.

I have already found a home,
and I want babies without wings, big beautiful oak trees,
and for our romantic parodies to be kept on-screen.

Cupid's got games,
but this girl plays her own way.

CATHERINE PITTS

247

A Letter to John Keats

Dear John Keats,

I was a caged bird
learning to hold a melody
flipping through the pages
of books I didn't want to read
(literary confessions)

musing on escape
and counting the years
of my tender age
so eager
for my days to pass

how I longed
to get older
so I could at least leave
but then I stumbled upon
your Ode to a Grecian Urn
"for ever warm and still to be enjoyed,
for ever panting, forever young—"

and I found myself
for the first time—captivated
by words written
hundreds of years
before my brief life

then I learned your story
the brevity of your pounding heart
and wondered about *"beauty is truth,"*
and *"who are these*
coming to the sacrifice"

and how
you did *so much*
with *so little* time
just 25 years—
25 years to make yourself remembered

and you gave me
the ambition
to do all I could
with each day I have
making the most of every moment

because though a poet's words
can become immortal
poets are not.

you gave me to fire
to escape my cage
armed only with a pen.

- Leigh

kindred spirits

though I am miles and miles
   from the place
I usually rest my head,
   I have found
a home tucked away in the
   tuscan countryside—
not the place, though it
   is lovely,
but with these people,
   these poets,
these artists, musicians,
   shared souls
whose hearts sing out
   to mine.
how is it that I can feel
   nostalgic
for a place I have not left?
   I dearly miss
the people sitting around me
   as I speak aloud
this ache in my chest, this
   breathless sorrow.
fortune smiles upon us,
   if only for
this shining moment—

we kindred spirits, we
   shared souls.

- Emma

My fingertips brush against the rust
that has made its home corroding
the corners of the iron gate.

A gentle push,
a high-pitched squeak,
an opportunity.

I step down and breathe in.
It smells cold and damp,
and my back eases,
spine relaxing as I take the first step.

Their voices echo around me
in the tunnels. Soft noises bouncing
from stone to stone, playing games with us.

Find me, they say.
Come and catch us.

I want to,
I reply.
But I'm not meant to stay.

FREYDIS LOVA

Quotes from Federica

"The more you travel the less you carry with you."

"I moved to Rome and became a barbarian driver."

"I will include some wine, is necessary."

"When you are born on the sea, it is hard to stay far."

"It's called common sense, but isn't always common."

"I think it's fun to do something you don't know how to do."

"To see an artwork is always something special,
to be in front of it."

"Even if it takes a bit longer, if you get lost it doesn't matter."

"This is a century of women."

"Italians are fun, for a love affair,
but you can't trust them."

"I have to be thankful, I have to live day by day,
I have to be grateful for when I am working."

Life happens in the places you go to fill up
and make you feel whole again,
Moments that make you feel most alive.

I will always search for strength
to carry on in places I feel like myself again.

The Great refining

It's crazy how much
we change through time…
our appearance, wants, desires.
It's hard to determine
the qualities that remain
and the ones that change,
what develops
and what is washed away.
I want to move with the wind
without losing my authenticity.
To do this, must I identify
what can fall away
and what must stay?

CATHERINE PITTS

XIV.

Tu me manques.
Aujord'hui et toujours.
Tu me manques.
J'espere que tu me vois.
Mais, tu ne me verrais que dans tes rêves.
Tu me manques.

You are missing me.
Today and always.
I miss you.
But you will only see me in your dreams.
You are missing me.

CAS MCDOWELL

256

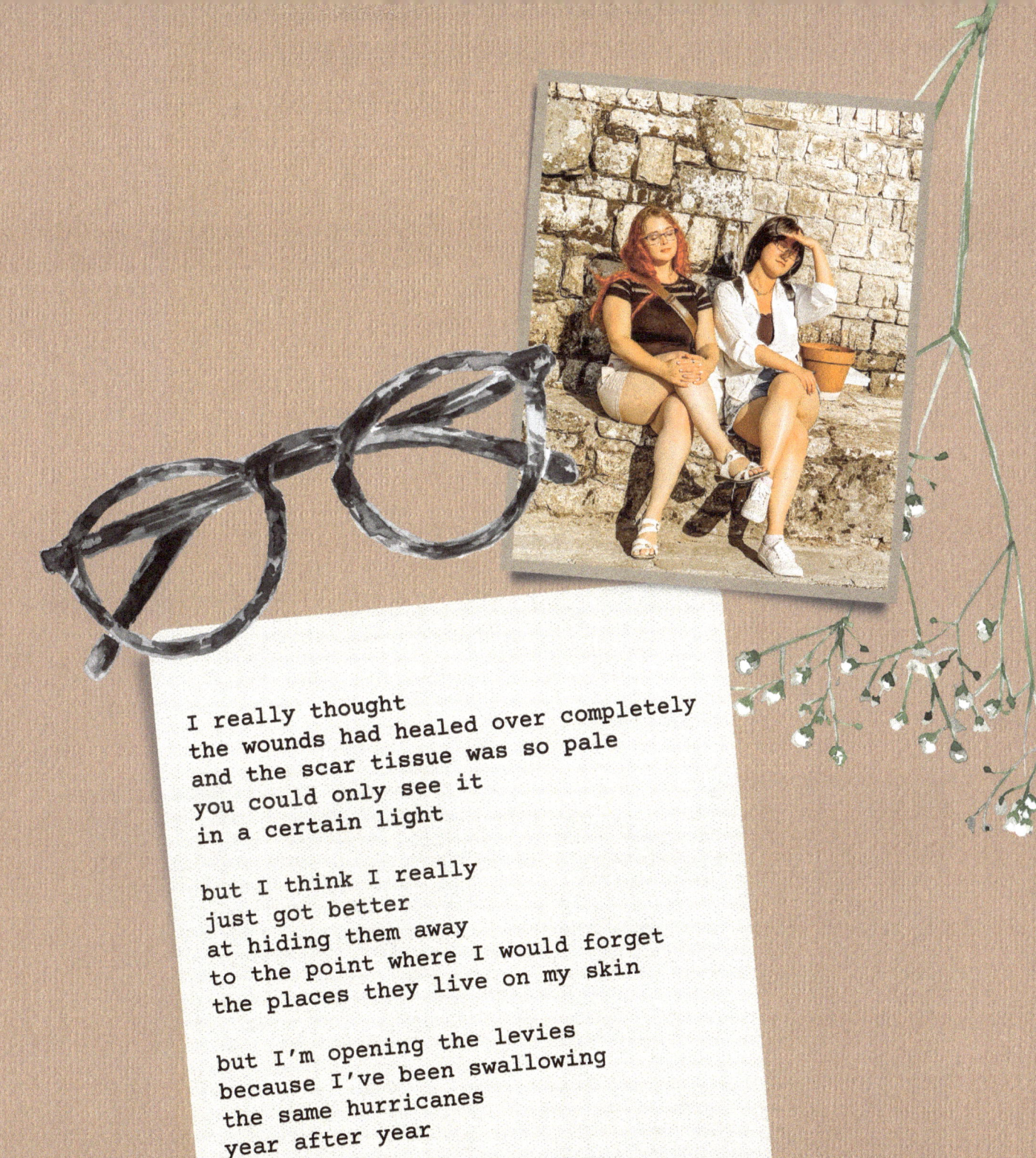

I really thought
the wounds had healed over completely
and the scar tissue was so pale
you could only see it
in a certain light

but I think I really
just got better
at hiding them away
to the point where I would forget
the places they live on my skin

but I'm opening the levies
because I've been swallowing
the same hurricanes
year after year

LEIGH FISHER

Aimless Lost Poets

Everyone here is a poet.
They are the most beautiful empathetic souls.
So young and brave, they are inspiring.
They get lost a lot and ask me to lead them home.

My aimless lost poets.
I am in awe right now.
Quietly enjoying each of them and the world around us.

Laura

Can I guess what color I'd use to paint your eyes? - Laura

I have room on my bookshelf for you. -Laura

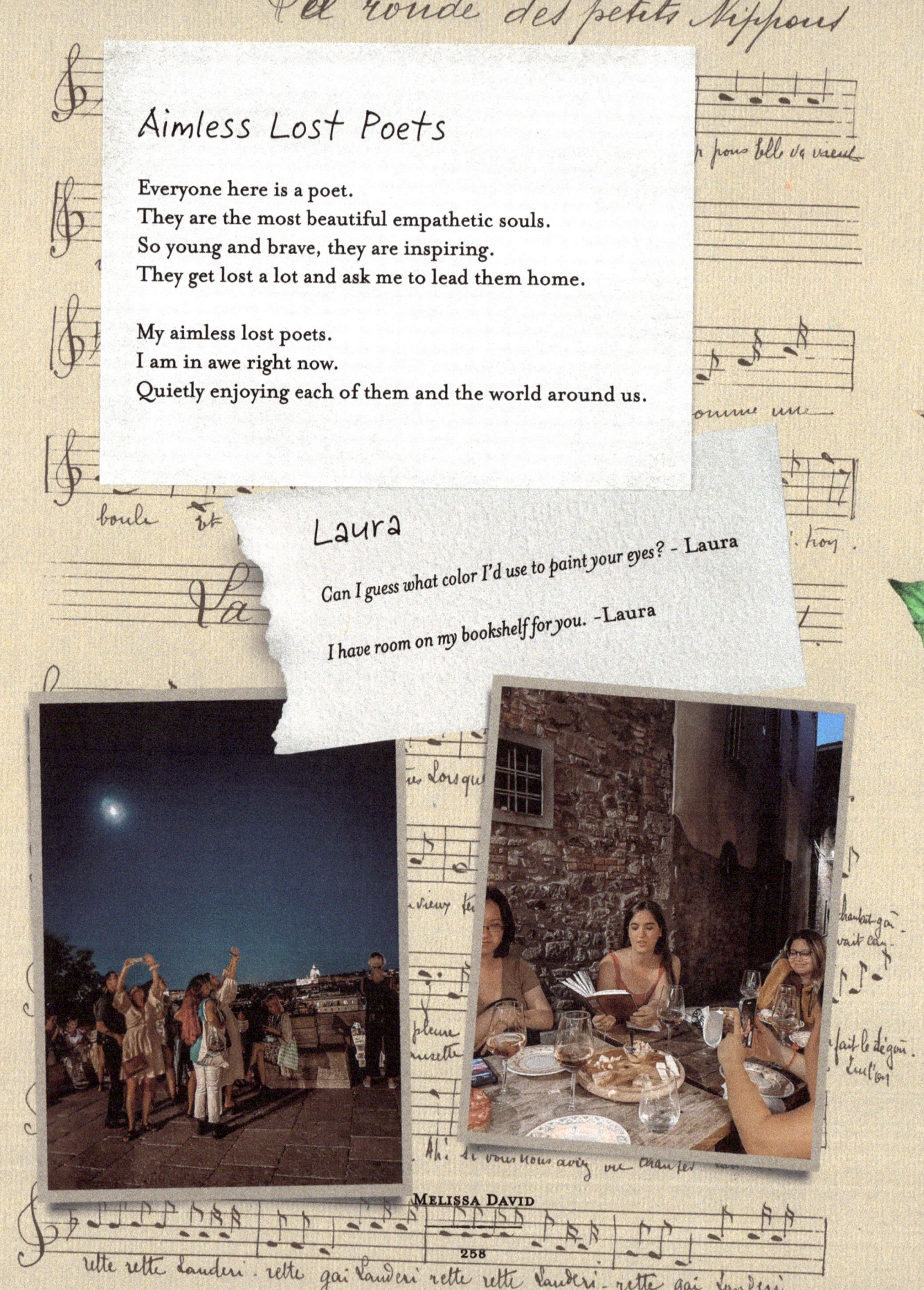

MELISSA DAVID

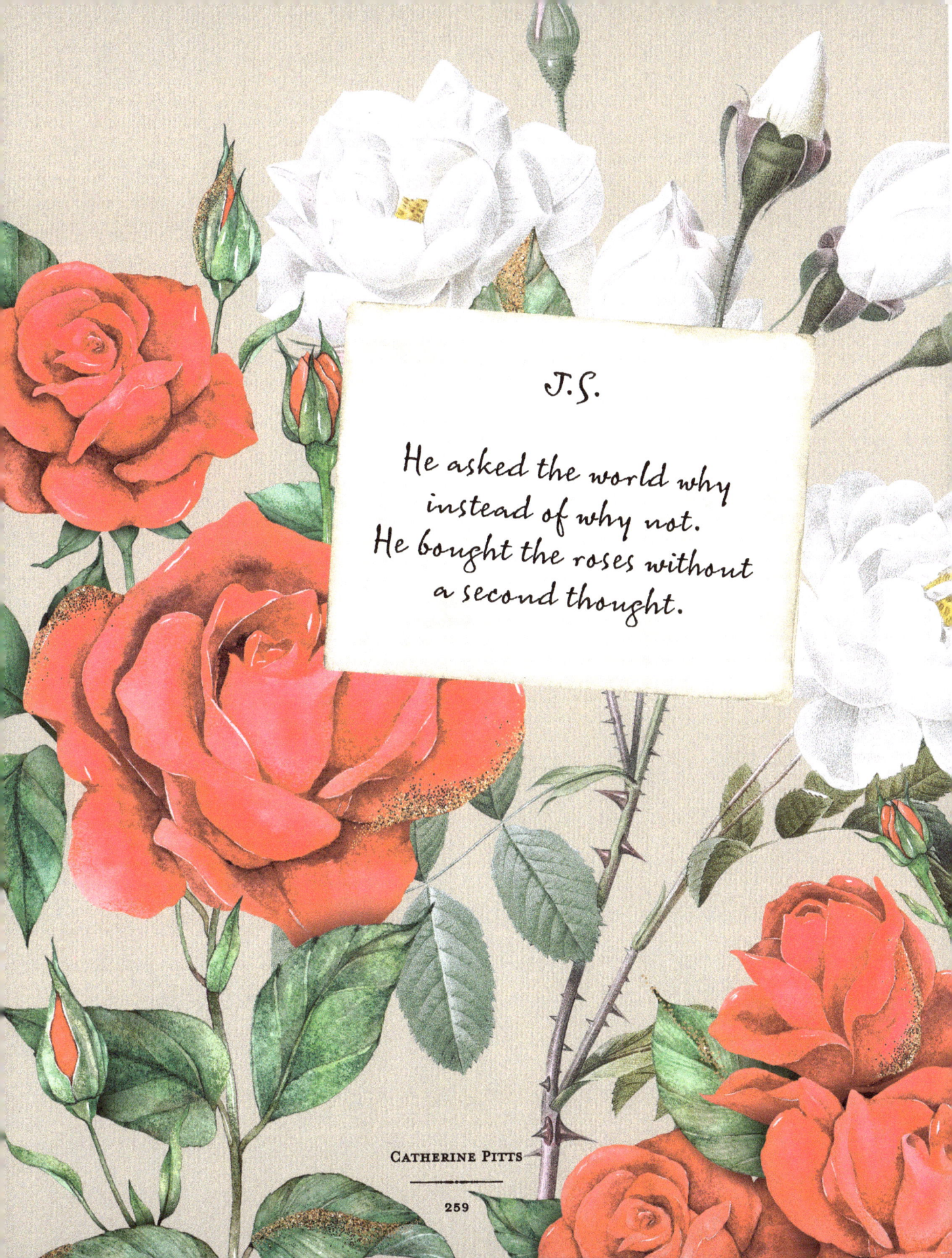

J.S.

He asked the world why
instead of why not.
He bought the roses without
a second thought.

CATHERINE PITTS

259

Last Night in Rome

tonight, I have witnessed
a new side of Rome—
Roma, Italia—
and I recall the words
of the bartender in Sorrento
mixing me cocktails
I couldn't afford
"un museo sotto il cielo"
"it's a museum under the sky,"
he said, with such passion
I truly believe
he meant it

even though he works
in a tourist town
and I grew up in a tourist town
where everything is fake
and kindness is mandatory
that falsity
feels so familiar
it's somehow made real
even with all that commonality
and the knowledge of bitterness—
I truly believe
he meant it

but in my first step
into that city of legend
I did not stray far enough
from common paths
to see its beauty
I existed in the common concourses
the places where every tourist
packs their body into a crowd
to see that sculpture—
to get into that Colosseum—
a dozen roses were thrust in my path
and I learned to duck the extended arms

LEIGH FISHER

but three years later
on a determined pilgrimage
on a journey to rediscover
the written word
with poets who now hold
my heart so dear
and to pay my respects to John Keats
with a single white rose
I keep stumbling across ruins
so beautiful in their splendor and height
reaching for the sky
for hundreds of years

everywhere I turn
there are more
and now I see the beauty
that bartender spoke of
and I feel the magic
that burns
in a city still living
full of lives, of stories
so long after it was built
not a ruin
but truly
a museum under the sky

LEIGH FISHER

8th july, 2022

today is the last day of the retreat. i'm starting to feel a little sombre, like i'm unconsciously preparing myself for when we part ways. my heart is only as strong as it could be on some days, but she's going to be a little fragile today. as i'm writing this on the bus, i can see everyone from my seat.

i'm trying to remember the simplicity of this moment, just all of us travelling. perhaps it doesn't matter where the destination is, as long as we're together.

映月

KAITLYN YÍNG YUÉ

July 9th

Rome

Before this trip— I was so often questioning why I do this. Why I am trying so hard to be a poet in a society that does not care for poets. It's because of this— it's for them.
<u>You are and always will be the reason</u>
<u>I will never stop trying.</u>

My pen is running out of ink— which is fitting. It is nearing the end of the most cosmic & magical week of my life. I am undone.

Our time together may be ending—
but this is only the beginning.

This is a rebirth.

My Sunflower Poets—
I am in the palm of the universe and
    you are my renaissance.

These next pages
are how poets say
goodbye...

It's 6:32 in the morning and I'm walking down my usual trail to watch the world slowly wake up. My mind can't help but wander back to cobblestones and a more simple life. In this moment, I had a calming effect wash over me, realizing this is the same sun rising over the Trevi. The same fountain I was standing at not too long ago with strangers who quickly became friends. Sharing laughs with people who resonated with me on another level. The sun takes its course as do I, falling into the illusion of time passing by.

But on this solitary walk, I find my heart elsewhere, back to our very first night.

DENAE TERESE

266

Every man should fear a brave woman
for there is nothing as fierce as she

J.S.

sunflowers

girasole,
bunga matahari,
太陽花,
sunflowers.

these are all the languages in which i know 'sunflower'.
little did i know, that this word would take on
a vast new meaning for me,
blooming tender and untouched,
fiercely facing the strength of the sun.

it now reminds me
of the warmth and resilience
that resides in the souls of
my kindred company.

true to the name
of the flower that
we've chosen as our symbol
i will remember them
in a sunflower's manner,
and look towards their faces,
because to me,
they are the sun.

* 太陽花 / tài-yáng huā *

KAITLYN YÍNG YUÉ

XVI. A boy with a stolen rose

Un ragazzo con la rosa rubata presents you with a hope and a dream. Un ragazzo who is more than just a fantasy. He's more than Darcy, d'Artagnan or Pan. He's imperfect. Un ragazzo and somehow this rose is the smallest glimpse of perfection. Ragazzo is found in you, and I truly hope it is a youth you never deny. Your love is big. It is good. Ragazzo, look and see how bright you shine.

CAS McDOWELL

a rebirth turning
straight towards
the light, the
Italians called
her Girasole

JENNIFER GELLOCK

271

Time to Go Home

On my way home I watched two lovers on the plane
watch a movie together
Each on their own individual movie screens
pressed play at the same exact time.
"One,
Two,
three
Press play".
They said as they looked at one another.
The film well on its way
It made me think -
How they both intentionally chose to have their two spirits
journey together on two parallel timelines.
An outsider would notice them living the same exact experience
However, their internal processes of that movie
must have been completely different
I watched her nod off and place her head
upon his shoulder two minutes in
I watched him slowly sipping red wine
engaged the whole time as he stroked her hair
Two people moving in the same direction yet,
never truly knowing how the other one feels

Do you think they discussed the plot-line together?

[NOTE: WRITTEN ON THE FLIGHT BACK HOME TO THE US]

JENNIFER GELLOCK

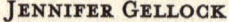

272

Worlds colliding

I'm watching my two worlds collide.
In my Italian notebook,
from my European bag,
I write.

With my iced coffee,
old journal and Florida driver's license beside me.
I sit on a wooden picnic table in downtown St. Pete,
Kendrick Lamar fills the airways,
I listen as people speak English next to me,
my mind still full of European slang,
I fully embrace this day.

I choose not to judge my current environment.
But rather, embrace who I am
in the midst of constant change
...mostly by the will of my own two feet.

CATHERINE PITTS

Traveling changes something in me
and I long to hold on to it
long after I am home

DENAE TERESE

Each night I found myself in a world
   of dreamless sleep

That was until I met her
Waking every morning to be lost
      in such magic that even dreams dare not know
Now she has left and so too
am I to wonder what was real and what was not

In this mystery my mind shall never find
any true answers but one

   She was real

         J.S.

J.S.
—————
275

It was the trip of a lifetime
Yet, a lifetime wasn't long enough
As the days transitioned effortlessly
One into another
It felt like a snapshot in time
A snowglobe turned upside down
Then slowly settling into place
I pray I never forget
The sunflowers
Piazzas
And poets
Of that one Italian week
in the heart of our summer

JENNIFER GELLOCK

9th july, 2022

last night was just a tearful goodbye. we took our usual walk after dinner and it just seemed to me that we're trying to steal away as much time as we could. at least, that was definitely how i felt. Rome, in all its glory, gave us a beautiful last night as a sendoff. the city never felt more vibrant and alive, and we looked at constellations and admired the sights. when we returned to the hotel and parted ways, i was the first to go. a part of me felt like if i hadn't left first, then i'd probably never would.

thankfully, i managed to see rachel, laura, mel and leigh one last time in the morning before i had to leave for the airport. i wasn't expecting it, but i'm so glad it happened. i felt my heart cave in from relief from seeing their familiar faces. last night felt too much like an ending. seeing them the next morning felt more like a semicolon, like i'll be waiting to see them again and continue our travels elsewhere. in the end, i'm able to go back home with a heart less heavy and more hopeful;

KAITLYN YÍNG YUÉ

13 sunflowers

the poet tells you about the sunflowers in her garden as you walk together after dinner / the poets pull out an extra pen when you need one / the poets write poems for each other / the poet sings so beautifully the vaulted ceilings ring like bells clattering together / the poets read their poems to one another in the atrium / the poets sit in the grass under the trees / the poet's pink hair matches the flowers, so the poet takes a picture of her / the poet calls you beautiful strangers / the poet writes a poem in swedish / the poet reads a poem that cracks you in two / the poet gives you a hug at breakfast, sensing the exact moment you need it / the poet shares her umbrella / the poets join you on your pilgrimage for your favorite pizza in florence / the poet buys you the quill pen you can't afford just to see you smile / the poet shares ravioli when they catch you looking / the poets eat breakfast together every morning, drifting in and out with the tides / the poets look at paintings together / the poets furiously jot down notes in their journals / the poets get a matching tattoos together / the poets talk of kindred spirits, sunflowers, a renaissance / the poet lends you a dramamine / the poet teaches oracle poetry in the sun-dappled afternoon / the poet teaches watercolor in the gardens / the poets tell you about their loves, past and present / the poet shares in your anger / the poet walks home with you / the poet buys a round of appetizers and wine / the poets toast the gift they have shared together / the poet reads the beautiful verses she dedicated to each of you on montecatini-alto / the poet brings you all together / the poets make you feel at home / and they always will.

EMMA CONLON

To

Rachel & Laura

(contains espresso...)

to rachel, who is
quickly becoming one of
my dearest friends

"Those we are fated to meet
shall guide us to that which we are
destined to do." -SS

for rachel, an earthly yet ethereal
muse.

she's the kind that lets tears fall
as words wishes to spill out
from her
she's the kind to pull you up
when you trip
fussing over your lightly
scraped knees and giving
you the warmest embrace.

for Laura:
There is a sweetness in her smile
that has also known grief and
pain that would tear a soul to
shreads. But she has taken the
ribbons of broken hearts and
set aside dreams, and wrapped up
her tomorrows with wishes and
warm hugs that mirror a Tuscan
sunrise, and given them to the souls
she has stitched together from the
farthest points of the earth, making
the globe feel just a little bit
smaller— and how wonderful is that,
that she can smile, and we can
feel her embrace from anywhere
in the world?

Rachel & Laura
You have changed
my life. I love
you both so so
much. Thank
you. ♡
-Me

This trip was everything
and more ♡ thank you
for reminding me what it
is like to live again.

you all hold a special place
in my heart for always ☺

Safe travels, xo
♡Jenna

Dear Rachel,

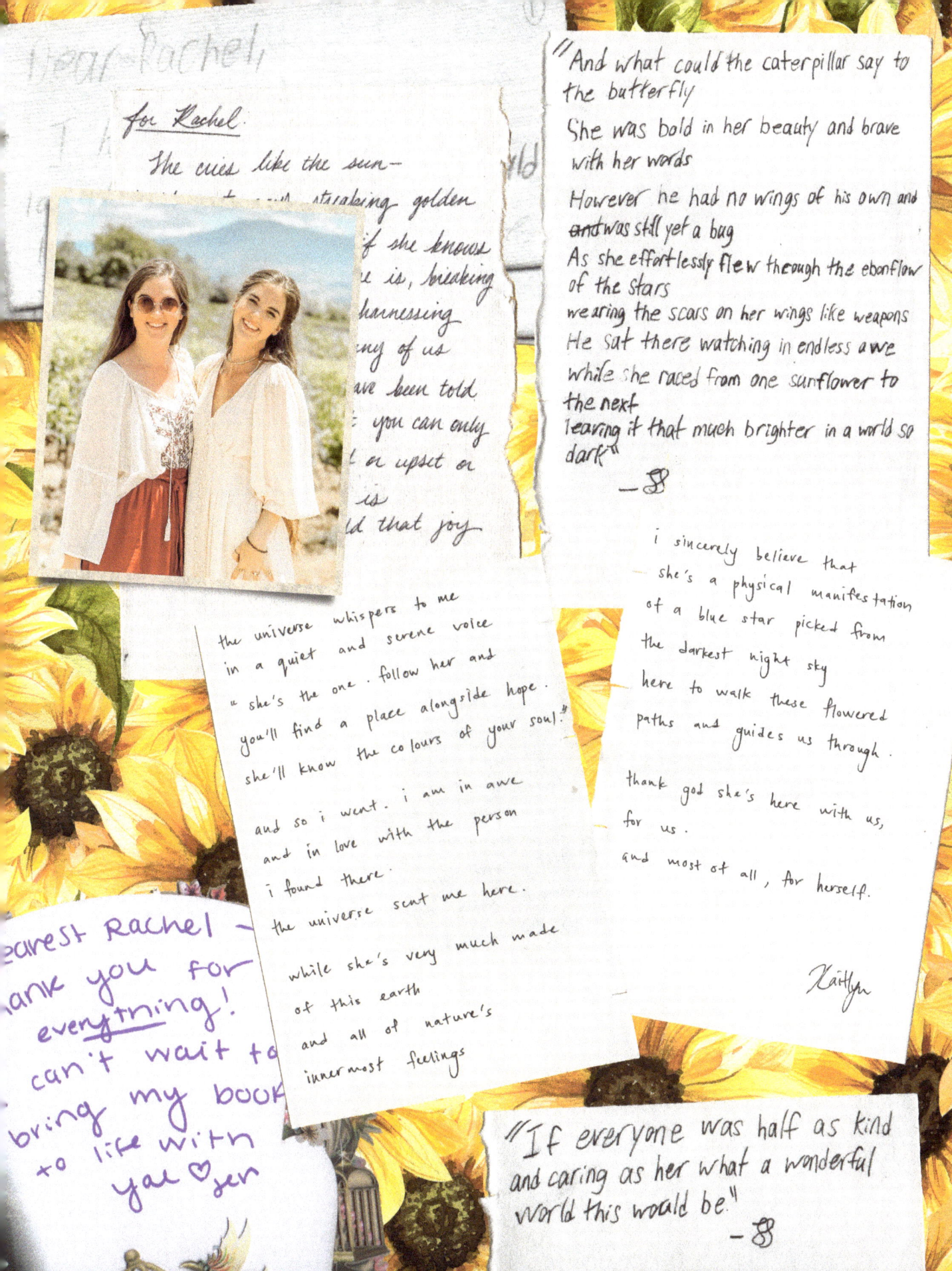

for Rachel:

She cries like the sun—
... ...streaking golden
... if she knows
... e is, breaking
... harnessing
... y of us
... ave been told
... you can only
... or upset or
... is
... d that joy

"And what could the caterpillar say to
the butterfly
She was bold in her beauty and brave
with her words
However he had no wings of his own and
~~and was still~~ yet a bug
As she effortlessly flew through the ebonflow
of the stars
wearing the scars on her wings like weapons
He sat there watching in endless awe
while she raced from one sunflower to
the next
leaving it that much brighter in a world so
dark"
— ❀

the universe whispers to me
in a quiet and serene voice
" she's the one. follow her and
you'll find a place alongside hope.
she'll know the colours of your soul."

and so i went. i am in awe
and in love with the person
i found there.
the universe sent me here.

while she's very much made
of this earth
and all of nature's
innermost feelings

i sincerely believe that
she's a physical manifestation
of a blue star picked from
the darkest night sky
here to walk these flowered
paths and guides us through.

thank god she's here with us,
for us.
and most of all, for herself.

Kaitlyn

Dearest Rachel ~
thank you for
everything!
can't wait to
bring my book
to life with
you ♡ Jen

"If everyone was half as kind
and caring as her what a wonderful
world this would be"
— ❀

You are my renaissance

I am in the palm of the universe and
you are my renaissance—

Emma, the one that is made of
changing tides and siren song.
You are my renaissance—
Malena, the one that embodies every gentle flower,
a breath of fresh air.
You are my renaissance—
Denae, the one who must choose courage,
who may be the bravest of us all.
You are my renaissance—
Kaitlyn, the one whose heart holds infinite love,
who will never give up.
You are my renaissance—
Cas, the one whose soul is ever
expanding, changing, learning.
You are my renaissance—
Catherine, the one with a smile like starlight,
who reminds me how important it is to dance in the rain.
You are my renaissance—
Jen, the one who has put down her armor
and picked up a pen, vulnerable and magnificent.
You are my renaissance—
J.S., the one that after so much time
has found a way to believe in magic.
You are my renaissance—
Leigh, the one with a voice like soft, soft velvet,
holding you close, keeping you warm.
You are my renaissance—
Mel, the one who sees me
for all that I am, and all I am meant to be.
You are my renaissance—
Freydis, the one that breathes in
inspiration and exhales poetry.

I am in the palm of the universe,
you are my renaissance,
and this is only the beginning.

Ever yours,
xx R.

_____

Find us beyond the page

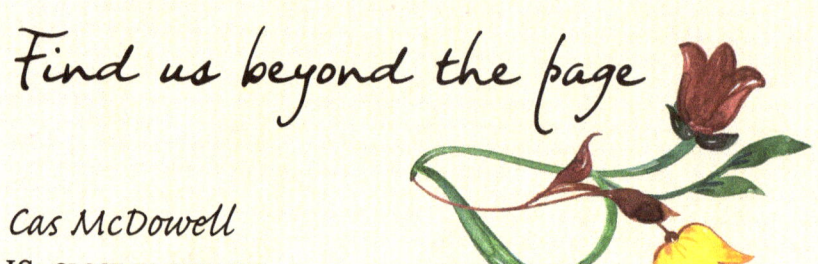

Cas McDowell
IG: @LOST.IN.ORVIETO

Catherine Pitts
IG: @CATHERINEPITTS

Denae Terese
IG: @D.TERESE_
DENAETERESE.COM

Emma Conlon
IG, FACEBOOK, TIKTOK: @BYEMMACONLON

Freydis Lova
IG: @FREYDIS.LOVA
FREYDISLOVAPOETRY.COM

J.S.
IG: @HEARTLESSNOMADPOETRY

Jennifer Gellock, Ph.D
IG: @JENNIFER_GELLOCK
@INWARDATHLETE
INWARDATHLETE.COM

Kaitlyn Yíng Yué

Malena Grace
IG: @MALENAGRACEPOETRY

Leigh Fisher
IG: @SLEEPLESSAUTHORESS

Melissa David
IG: @MELISSADAVIDENTERPRISES
MELISSADAVID.COM

L. A. Clift
IG: @L.A.CLIFT
LAURACLIFT.COM

R. Clift
IG: @R.CLIFTPOETRY
RCLIFTPOETRY.COM

Scan for links to poetry books
written by my Sunflower Poets!

Thank you for being
my renaissance.

Until we meet again...
All my love,
xx R.

DIGITAL ARCHIVE OF PHOTOS, VIDEOS, & MORE

ISBN: 978-1-960045-07-2 (paperback),
978-1-960045-08-9 (hardback).

Book design & layout by Rachel Clift.
Cover design by Rachel Clift.
rcliftpoetry.com

First printing edition, 2023.

Travel Itinerary organized and operated by TrovaTrip
and G2 Travel.
trovatrip.com

www.ingramcontent.com/pod-product-compliance
Lightning Source LLC
Chambersburg PA
CBHW041544120626
46551CB00019B/2835